W9-AFG-833

Carers' Stories

Carers' Stories:
Walking Alongside a Person with Dementia

By

Gill Constable

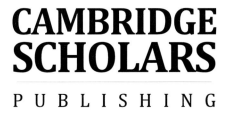

CAMBRIDGE
SCHOLARS
PUBLISHING

Carers' Stories: Walking Alongside a Person with Dementia,
by Gill Constable

This book first published 2013

Cambridge Scholars Publishing

12 Back Chapman Street, Newcastle upon Tyne, NE6 2XX, UK

British Library Cataloguing in Publication Data
A catalogue record for this book is available from the British Library

ISBN (10): 1-4438-5149-3, ISBN (13): 978-1-4438-5149-7

This book is dedicated to the carers that gave so generously of their time. They revisited events that were often emotionally challenging for them. Their motivation in doing so was so that we could learn from their experiences, so that the needs of people with dementia and their carers could be better understood and met.

I want to thank Gill Clarke and Melanie Nind for their scholarly guidance throughout the research process.

I am very grateful to my partner Isla Duncan for her constant support, patience, wisdom and encouragement, which has made the publication of this book a reality.

TABLE OF CONTENTS

LIST OF FIGURE AND TABLES

INTRODUCTION

This book focuses on the experiences undertaken by carers supporting someone with dementia. It has been written using a biographical approach of caring, which places caring within a social, cultural and personal context. It considers how change is managed and the coping strategies utilised; how carers developed their understanding of what is important in life, and made sense of their experiences. The role of health and social care services was reflected upon by the carers, who identified what was unhelpful, as well as supportive and effective practice and resources.

By hearing these stories we can enhance our knowledge and understanding of how to best support carers and by doing so support the person with dementia. The term carer is used to describe a family member or friend who is caring for someone based on their relationship rather than a paid carer. I have used a biographical or life story approach to frame the experiences of carers, as this is person centred and recognises the unique individuality of people. The audience for this book is anyone who supports a person with dementia in a paid or unpaid capacity, or has a role in the provision or commissioning of services and wants to understand better the legislative and policy context for carers, as well as the strategies that support people with dementia to maintain a sense of identity and wellbeing. Living alongside a person with dementia helps us to develop knowledge about what is really important in people's lives, including our own, and what gives joy and contentment. It challenges the notion that all care giving is a burden and that supporting people with dementia is tragic with dire consequences for the care giver (Netto, Goh and Yap, 2009).

This work is significant to me as I teach students who are training to be social workers. Increasingly social work practice in local authorities involves safeguarding adults with special needs. People with cognitive impairments are especially vulnerable to emotional, financial, sexual and physical abuse, as well as neglect (Pritchard, 2007). People are made vulnerable not by their needs but by the environments they find themselves in and the services they receive:

it is societal processes which create vulnerability. People who are called 'vulnerable adults' may be in need of community services to enjoy independence, but this is not what makes them vulnerable. What makes them vulnerable is the way they are treated by society generally and more specifically by those that support them. Vulnerability is therefore also a particular form of oppression (Martin, 2007: 16).

This has been confirmed by my experience. One of my first jobs as a young person was working in a care home for older people. A significant proportion of the residents had dementia. The care home was a large Victorian house arranged on three storeys, entirely unsuitable for older people with mobility difficulties as there was no lift, and therefore no access to a garden or the world outside. The female residents were on the floor above the men. I was allocated to the women's floor which was referred to by some staff as the "babies' floor", which was highly demeaning and stigmatising. The women shared large rooms which accommodated up to four people. The floor was linoleum and the environment sparse and bleak. These women were state funded and afforded no privacy or dignity. The routines of the home were inflexible and boring. Even to this day I can remember the women's names and I felt a great sense of affection for them. They were highly individual, and the factor of their dementia did not diminish this. My memory contains sadness, as they deserved much better care. They were abandoned by family and friends, as there were few visitors. Some of the care assistants were emotionally disengaged and assumed that acts of frustration and aggression were premeditated by the residents rather than indicators of distress. These staff could be critical and disparaging towards the residents, as if their cognitive impairments made them less than human. Many of these attitudes stemmed from a lack of knowledge and understanding about people's needs, as no training was provided, but I remember three members of staff in particular, who were young like me and very kind in their treatment of the residents. To see this type of compassion in practice in an environment that was the antithesis of homely was significant for me, as I wanted to be like those staff.

My experience in that care home many years ago gave me a profound and enduring insight into the importance of empathy in the support provided to people with dementia (Sheard, 2007).The quality of care is sadly still highly variable, and a lack of emotional closeness and interaction has been identified, as a continuing cause for concern in the support that people with dementia experience (Commission for Social Care Inspection, 2008). This led in 2009 to the publication of the National Dementia Strategy in

England. It highlighted that people with dementia living in the community require their carers to be supported by health and social care services and is cross-referenced to the Carers Strategy (Department of Health, 2008a). Carers are entitled to have their needs assessed, and to be supported to remain in employment, education and able to participate in leisure activities, as well as provided with short term breaks from caring. Since 1995 there have been three pieces of legislation as well as policy building on the entitlements of carers to be supported in their role. The current Coalition Government has broadly supported recent policy both in terms of people with dementia and carers (Department of Health, 2010a, 2010c). In spite of the legislative and policy framework to support carers, services are inconsistent and inadequate due to a lack of political priority given to carers (Carers UK, 2009). These factors added to my interest in this area given that carers receive inadequate information, advice, emotional and practical support from the state. I was curious to understand more about the emotional resilience that enabled carers to maintain a relationship with the person with dementia, as the illness progressed, which inevitably resulted in the relationship changing with the cared for person becoming more dependent.

There is considerable public interest and concern about dementia in the UK, which is proportionately affecting more people as the British population ages, as its prevalence increases with longevity (Department of Health, 2009). It is estimated that there are 750,000 people living with dementia and 500,000 partners, family members and friends are involved in caring for someone with dementia at a value of £6 billion a year, if care was provided by health and social care services (Department of Health, 2009).

I wanted to understand about the lived experience of being an informal, unpaid carer, the coping approaches that family members or friends used; the resilience they developed to go on caring; their views of health and social care services, whether they felt partners in the co-production of care (Needham and Carr, 2012). I wanted issues of diversity to be reflected in terms of sexuality, so I ensured that I heard the stories of carers who identified as lesbian or gay. I wished to capture the particular experiences of this group, which generally is neglected in research (Turnball, 2002). It is important not to assume carers are all the same with similar needs; consequently one aspect of the research was to discover if the carers had found health and social care services "gay friendly" (Age UK, 2010). Heterosexism in my experience is often implicit in health and social care services, and I wished to give lesbian and gay carers a presence in the book. This was not just in recognition of their existence, but more a positive validation of the emotional and practical contribution that they too make as carers. It is my belief that there is more commonality between people than differences, and being a carer illustrates this point. For example one lesbian carer speaking of supporting her partner with dementia described it as: "like walking on thin ice and the ice is getting thinner and thinner but you don't especially notice – until suddenly you fall through, and your world is suddenly so, so very different" (Dixey, 2010:49). This powerful image expresses loss and fear by using ice as a simile, and could probably be expressed by many carers irrespective of their sexuality. Nevertheless for lesbian women and gay men they may experience discrimination, marginalisation and invalidation of their relationships due to their sexuality, which only makes caring more fraught and distressing. For these reasons their stories should be heard.

There is a need for a shift from medical approaches to dementia to person centred thinking and practice, which recognises the importance of maintaining personhood through curiosity and knowledge about people's biographies. The aim is to enable practice to be inclusive and gay friendly by recognising the importance of life stories, and consequentially valuing the knowledge carers hold about the person with dementia. This enables a sense of identity to be sustained, and enhances well-being; moreover it offers person centred practice to both the carer and the person with dementia. We will now explore the impact of dementia, the experience of ageing and sexuality.

CHAPTER ONE

DEMENTIA, AGEING AND SEXUALITY

Introduction

This chapter explores dementia, ageing and sexuality. I have adapted Erben's (1998: 7) schema for biographical research, as this provides a framework that enables me to reflect on the lives of carers within their social, political, cultural and personal contexts. I have adopted a dyadic approach where the relationship between the person with dementia and their carer is understood as one of interdependency, where personal histories and identities are seen as co-existing (Brooker, 2007; Piiparinen and Whitlatch, 2011). I critically examine different theoretical and policy approaches to dementia and ageing in order to enhance understanding of the experience of caring in the context of supporting someone with dementia, in contrast to another disability. The incidence of dementia increases with age, so theories of ageing and social policy perspectives pertaining to old age are explored.

There is a focus on lesbian women and gay men as carers, as often heterosexist and familial assumptions are made about caring and the life styles that people have experienced (Harrison, 2006; Fannin *et al.*, 2008). These will be addressed by examining the "cultural system, societal context and chronology" of caring (Erben,1998: 7). In the following chapters we will then move onto the "specific events" and "local context" to explore issues of identity, resilience and coping strategies adopted by carers. The intention is to acknowledge both the challenges and rewards of caring, as carers "protect people with dementia from potential harms of society, a society that fears deviance and disorder, and craves control and conformity to the cultural 'norms', a set of fears and values that dementia undermines" (Innes, 2009: 61).

The importance of being present for the person with dementia "… letting go of the constant doing involved in dementia care and become involved in being with the person" to sustain a sense of their identity and well-being (Mackinlay and Trevitt, 2012: 206). This is achieved through an understanding of the person's biography, their interests, preferences and skills, so that their illness does not become their identity, resulting in labelling and social exclusion (Kitwood, 1997).

Using Erben's Schema of Biographical Research

I have adapted the schema developed by Erben (1998: 7) to provide a framework to map the journey of people with dementia and carers. The rationale for its adoption is that it firmly locates the individual within their social context, and provides a systematic process of ensuring that the carers' narratives are evaluated against the backdrop of the time in which they are living.

Figure 1-1: Biographical Schema for Carers

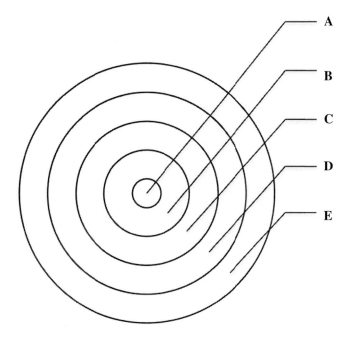

Key

A: Specific events   **B:** Local context   **C:** Societal context
D: Cultural system   **E:** Chronology
Adapted from Erben (1998: 7)

The Schema is used so we can review the:

- Societal context and cultural systems impacting on the notion of caring and dementia, set within a chronology.
- Specific events and local context of the personal experience and challenges of caring with reference to identity, sexuality and coping strategies.

Prevalence of Dementia

Dementia is a collective term for a syndrome that causes a range of illnesses which impact on the cognitive abilities of the person, resulting in the decline of memory, reasoning, communication skills and the capacity to undertake daily living activities. The condition is enduring and progressive. People may develop behavioural and psychological symptoms such as depression, psychosis, aggression and wandering. It is estimated that there are 750,000 people with dementia in the UK; two thirds live in the community, while a third live in care homes and 64% of people in care homes have dementia (Alzheimer's Society, 2010). The numbers of people with dementia are set to increase to 1.4 million in the next 30 years (Department of Health, 2009). The likelihood of acquiring dementia increases with age, which is the one consistent predictor of the illness. Table 1.1 sets out the prevalence rates of dementia that demonstrate the linkage between age and the illness.

Table 1.1: Prevalence Rates of Dementia According to Age

Age	Prevalence Rates
40 – 65 years	1 in 1,000 people
65 – 70 years	1 in 50 people
70 – 80 years	1 in 20 people
80 years +	1 in 5 people

(Commission for Social Care Inspection, 2008a)

Only one third of people with the condition ever receive a diagnosis. Cheston and Bender (1999) argue, based on research in the UK, that this is due largely to the stigma of the illness, and to ageism. Williamson (2008) found that 50% of people in Britain believe a diagnosis of dementia is stigmatising. The writer Terry Pratchett, speaking about his own diagnosis of dementia, said: "It is a strange life; when you 'come out' people get embarrassed, lower their voices, get lost for words" (Williamson, 2008: ix).

The use of the term "coming out" has been adopted by lesbian women and gay men when they tell families, friends and work colleagues of their sexual identity. A participant in the Gay and Grey research project in Dorset said: "Coming out is a continuous process of negotiation and deciding on a daily basis as to whether it is worth the risk of revealing myself" (Fannin *et al.*, 2008: 14). The decision to "come out" about a diagnosis of dementia is similar, as the person will assess the risks as opposed to the benefits, and how other people will react to them (Harrison, 2006; Scholl and Sabat, 2008). This is an issue of social justice where people experience a sense of anxiety if they disclose pertinent issues pertaining to their sexual identity or health needs.

Mackenzie's (2006) research involving twenty-one carers from East European and South Asian communities in the north of England highlighted the impact of stigma that resulted in reluctance to identify dementia and access services. The consequence was that carers adopted coping approaches that were specific to their cultural norms. For example in the South Asian community there is no word for dementia, so the term "memory problems" was used. In these communities religious ideology also meant that the person with dementia was seen as being punished for misdeeds in a previous life and their current reincarnation was viewed as evidence of this. In the Polish and Ukrainian communities the extreme suffering experienced during the Second World War had resulted in a culture where: "Sharing inner feelings with people outside of a close family group becomes an invasion of the other's private space and invades their strategies for managing the lasting effects of trauma in their own biographies" (Mackenzie, 2006: 239).

The coping strategies used were to explain the condition as a physical illness, and, when this was no longer feasible, to isolate the person with dementia from the wider community. Another approach was to maintain an appearance of normal life. One Polish husband would accompany his wife with dementia to a day centre, so the neighbours thought they were going out together. It provided the husband with the opportunity to be in a "dementia safe environment" (Mackenzie, 2006: 242) where he could relax and socialise with other people. The fear of stigma beyond the immediate family caused considerable anxiety. Because of the small sample of carers, these findings cannot be generalised to the wider communities, but nonetheless they afforded valuable insights.

Conceptualising Dementia

Innes (2009) points out that the academic study of dementia has taken place around three theoretical perspectives: biomedical, social-psychological or psycho-social and social-gerontological. These approaches influence how people with dementia are supported. The biomedical approach sees dementia as a progressive disease and focuses on the declining abilities of people to undertake tasks required for daily living, and therefore is a deficit model. Social-psychological approaches see the maintenance of personhood as paramount, and incorporate the person's biography and personality to maintain personhood through empathetic care that enhances well-being. Social-gerontological perspectives include social, economic and political factors and assess how they determine the experience of ageing in different societies.

Ballenger (2008:494) argues that dementia has been 'framed' throughout history:

> Frames are the concepts and metaphors that allow human beings to understand reality, transforming the indecipherable complexity into a comprehensive pattern that we can recognize. Frames shape what counts as common sense, and as a result they shape our goals, and our plans and actions for reaching them.

How dementia has been understood impacts on the treatment provided; support given to carers, and the development and implementation of social policy. O'Connor *et al.* (2007) argue that a framework for dementia research should comprise: the subjective experience of the person with dementia; the immediate environment and its impact on social relationships; and the socio-cultural context in terms of how dementia is socially constructed. However, seeking a cure for the illness has been the priority for research in the USA and UK rather than providing high quality support for people with dementia and their carers. Kitwood (1997: 43) vividly demonstrates that:

> Medical approaches in psychiatry have, however, brought their own problems ... simplistic views of organicity, research led not so much by theory as available technique, and exaggerated hopes that science will deliver wonder-cures. Often personhood has been disregarded, particularly

when the 'patients' cannot easily speak in support of their own interests. It has become all too easy to ignore the suffering of fellow human beings and see instead a merely biological problem, to be solved by some kind of technical intervention.

The medicalisation of dementia has resulted in people frequently being provided with care that is underpinned by "malignant social psychology" (Kitwood, 1997: 45; Doherty *et al.*, 2009) that fails to recognise the human need for social interaction, emotional warmth and validation. Furthermore, Kitwood suggests that this has led to the inappropriate use of medication to reduce behaviour that is challenging rather than seeing it as an expression of an emotional need. Means *et al.* (2008) argue on the basis of UK research that the priority for health research funding has been into acute rather than chronic health conditions, and there has been "a long history of neglect" (p.21) of services for older people resulting in "family members that have long shouldered the burdens of caregiving ... finding it difficult to access services that help them continue to provide care" (Ballenger, 2008: 505).

This leads to service shortfalls or provision that does not meet the needs of the person with dementia and their carer, such as a lack of diagnosis, and therefore inadequate or inappropriate treatment. Insufficient community-based services including respite care have led to early long term admission to care homes. The Alzheimer's Society (Quince, 2011) surveyed 2,000 carers, people with dementia and care home workers about their experience of dementia services in the community, and found that 52% of carers said they received insufficient support. This resulted in 63% of carers stating that this had a negative impact on their general health, and culminated in the person with dementia being admitted to a care home earlier than necessary, as well as leading to unnecessary admission to hospital, in spite of the fact that 83% of all respondents stressed that being able to continue living at home was very important to the person with dementia. Furthermore domiciliary care services can be task orientated and inflexible without taking into account the person's needs or preferences, or that of the carer (Quince, 2011). Antipsychotic drugs have been used inappropriately in hospital and care homes to manage behaviour rather than assessing if the behaviour was due to pain, physical illness or anxiety. This type of medication can double the risk of death, triple the risk of having a stroke and hasten cognitive decline, and is inappropriate in the treatment of dementia (Banerjee, 2009). For people to receive inappropriate or incorrect treatment is an abuse of their human rights. People with dementia can be excluded from services such as Intermediate

Care Schemes (Commission for Social Care, 2008a; Department of Health, 2009). These services prevent hospital admission, support hospital discharge, provide re-enablement and rehabilitation services.

Biomedical ideologies that see dementia as a progressive disease can develop into cultures of care that are maintained by the power of the medical profession, the privatisation of care services and the interests of pharmaceutical companies (Kitwood, 1997). Such attitudes fail in the main to respond to people with dementia and carers at an emotional level where "feelings matter most" (Sheard, 2008: 48). The cultures of many care homes are institutional and the model of care is poorly defined. People with a diverse range of needs are placed together in an environment with "elements of a hospital, prison, hotel and a person's own home … [which] often become muddled into a care home" (Sheard, 2009: 60).

The first policy strategy for dementia in England and Wales was launched by the Department of Health in 2009. It seeks to reduce the stigma of the illness, provide early intervention to diagnosis, enhance the quality of services through improved support to carers, and provide better training of the workforce. The strategy follows the trajectory of the illness from diagnosis to end of life care. The title of the strategy and also underlying theme is the concept of "living well" with dementia by challenging the stigma that prevents discussion of dementia. This can induce feelings of isolation and helplessness. The strategy places an emphasis on enabling people to better understand the illness, and the resources and services that support people with dementia and their carers. Common understandings of dementia and their impact are presented by Figure 1.2 that has been taken from the strategy.

The diagram illustrates myths about dementia such as that it is a normal part of ageing, and that there is nothing that can be done to ameliorate its impact. This results in the condition not being diagnosed at its outset, which reduces people's capacity to plan for their future. The National Dementia Strategy (2009) challenges these misconceptions and is entitled "Living Well with Dementia". There is now far more public discussion of the illness but in my experience there is still considerable fear and misunderstanding about the illness. This needs to be addressed as it is estimated that 500,000 partners, family members and friends are involved in caring for someone with dementia (Department of Health, 2009). The National Dementia Strategy (2009) stipulates that the "Carers at the Heart of the 21st Century Strategy" (Department of Health, 2008a) is implemented

Figure 1-2: Current Understandings of Dementia

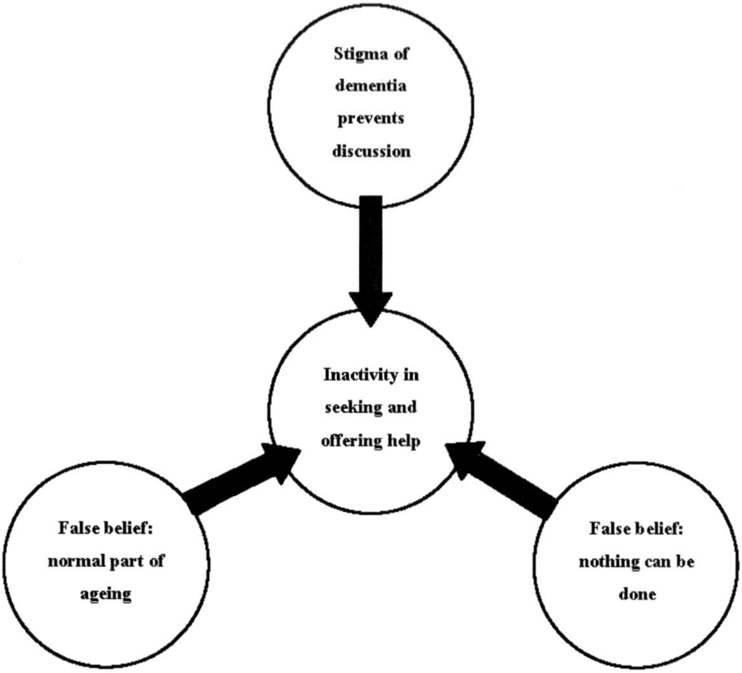

(Department of Health, 2009: 26)

for carers of people with dementia. The commitments include information and advice that are relevant to where the carer lives; short break provision; increased integration of health and social care services; GP provided health checks for carers, and opportunities for carers to take up paid employment and educational opportunities. Furthermore it outlines improvements to services that offer emotional support, as well as more targeted support to young carers with the provision of training for carers, to enable them to undertake their role and empower them to work with professionals. The Carers' Strategy acknowledges that little is known about lesbian, gay, bisexual and transgendered carers, but does not address this further. Recent Department of Health policy stresses whole family approaches, carers as experts and the importance of personalised support for carers and the cared for. Issues of diversity are not addressed (Department of Health, 2010c, HM Government, 2010).

In the next section I consider ideologies of ageing and how these inform "societal contexts and cultural systems" for people with dementia and carers (Erben, 1998: 7). This contextualises the experience of ageing and gives a critical overview as to the possible reasons why traditional dementia services that provide "dehumanising care practice" are able to develop, and have not been eradicated (Brooker, 2007: 15).

Ideologies of Ageing

As dementia is a condition that particularly impacts on older people, carers are invariably older too if they are partners or middle aged offspring. The process of ageing affects everyone, but it is debatable as to how it should be defined. Lives are structured by chronological age although the meanings given to different ages are socially constructed as a result of societal complexity, political and cultural diversity. As such, old age does not have a universal definition, but is dependent on the cultural and social context of the person, and their own understanding of old age (Dalrymple and Burke, 2006; Hughes, 2006).

The most common definition used in the organisation and delivery of education, health and social care services is chronological. In western societies people are allocated to particular services on the basis of both need and age. Retirement from work for the majority of people occurs in their sixties, and occupational and state pensions then become available. How age is defined in the UK is determined by organisational factors that are designed (in theory) to ensure an effective and efficient infrastructure. Definitions of old age do change over time for political and economic reasons. An increasingly ageing population will create demands for people to work longer, and older people to support each other even more than they do now (Tanner and Harris, 2008).

Life expectancy in the UK is currently 81 years for women and 77 years for men, in contrast to sub-Saharan Africa where the average age on death is the early 40s (Lawrence and Simpson, 2009). This statistic is startling and demonstrates the scale of global inequality. Being old in sub Saharan Africa will not be understood in the same way as being old in the UK. In addition far fewer people will be affected by dementia due to the lower life expectancy.

Age discrimination can be defined as discriminatory attitudes; behaviour and inequalities in terms of entitlements; choices and services towards people based on age. It can affect younger people as well as older people.

> Age is a social division; it is a dimension of the social structure on the basis of which power, privilege and opportunities tend to be allocated. Age is not just a simple matter of biological maturation – it is a highly significant social indicator (Thompson, 2001: 88).

Causes of age discrimination are related to economic factors in capitalism. Citizens are valued as workers: if not in paid employment people are perceived as not contributing. Culturally, older people are seen as taking health and social care resources from other sectors of the population (Tanner and Harris, 2008). Older people are regarded as a burden because of ageing populations in the western world, and these sentiments are expressed by terms such as "an ageing world" or "global greying" (Graham, 2007: 144). Such a view ignores the contributions that older people make to their families, friends and communities. Discrimination can focus on interpersonal factors with older people being thought as the "other", because of fears about ageing and death.

Age discrimination is now unlawful in employment, education and training (The Employment Equality (Age) Regulations 2006) , and consequently the retirement age has changed. It is less about social justice and more a response to an increasingly ageing population, with governments needing to reduce spending on pensions, benefits and public services (Tanner and Harris, 2008). Age discrimination means that people are denied the rights that other citizens have on the basis of age, whereas ageism identifies oppressive attitudes, values and beliefs that are culturally reinforced and impact negatively on the well-being of older people.

The concept of old age is often disparaged and not accorded respect. Harrison (2006: 44) makes links between dual oppressions:

> [D]iscussions of ageing frequently centre around costs, fears and even 'tidal waves' which conjure up notions of impending doom and gloom. Rarely are older people regarded as a resource, a source of positive societal input, or a demographic cohort of which to be proud. Ageism itself impacts on social and political understandings around the construction of age as something to be feared and avoided, rather than celebrated. In this respect, ageism and homophobia share common characteristics.

Furthermore a series of cultural assumptions is made about older people that encapsulate ageism (Thompson, 2001; Drummond, 2006; Harrison, 2006). When these cultural assumptions are applied to people with dementia they replicate aspects of the seventeen elements of "malignant social psychology … treachery, disempowerment, infantilization, intimidation, labelling, stigmatization, outpacing, invalidation, banishment, objectification, ignoring, imposition, withholding, accusation, disruption, mockery and disparagement" developed by Kitwood (1997: 46- 47), which reflect how people with dementia can be treated. I have added to the cultural assumptions developed by Thompson (2000: 90) in relation to people with dementia.

- "Old equals useless" – this links with economic factors that perpetuate age discrimination. Older people are seen as unproductive. This assumption fails to acknowledge the contribution that older people make within their families and the community such as being grandparents, carers, volunteers, consumers.

- "Old equals childlike" – this can result in older people being infantilised, when their experience, knowledge and skills are not recognised, valued or fully utilised (Askham *et al.*, 2007).

- "Old equals ill" – here health needs are put down to old age, and therefore health complaints are not taken seriously and treatment not provided.

- "Old equals not ill" – ailments are assessed as due to old age and therefore not worth treating. For example only one third of people with dementia obtain a diagnosis and are provided with appropriate treatment. This results in people not being able to make choices or plans for their future (Department of Health, 2009).

- "Old equals lonely" – such a view ignores older people's networks and contacts, and it assumes that older people do not make new friends. Loneliness is clearly not just experienced by some older people it can affect many people at different stages of life including the young.

- "Old equals unintelligent" – older people can be seen as slower in their comprehension and this misconception can lead to a

patronising approach, and assumptions made that older people are
confused and unreliable when providing information. This
concept gets played out in common sayings such as, "I am just
having a grey moment", as an explanation for forgetting a piece
of information.

- "Old equals inhuman" – by placing older people in a separate
  category through the use of terms such as "the elderly", "elderly
  mentally infirm", or "geriatrics".

- "Old equals poor" – while a significant number of older people
  live in poverty there are over five million people of retirement
  age living abroad many of whom have migrated with amassed
  wealth and occupational pensions (Lawrence and Simpson,
  2009). An assumption of poverty can prevent older people
  accessing choices and options such as purchasing support
  services privately that can enhance and maximise their
  independence.

- "Old equals asexual" - a belief that older people have no interest
  in sex (Phillips and Marks, 2006). Lesbian, gay or bisexual
  people have a sense of identity and community, which is more
  than sexual orientation (Commission for Social Care Inspection,
  2008b). Sexuality is part of being human and to deny this in older
  people is to treat them as less than human.

Older people can internalise feelings of ageism and experience a loss of
self-esteem. This will impact on their sense of identity: "no self or
personal experience story is ever an individual production" (Denzin, 1989:
73). Cultural assumptions can become beliefs held by older people and if
partly confirmed by how older people are treated by others they become
self-narratives, and this has particular implications for people with
dementia. To illustrate this point, Richards *et al.* (2007) analysed data
from 30 interviews with health and social care staff and found that their
understanding about older people was founded on personal experience and
practice without reference to theoretical or research based knowledge of
ageing and old age. This is likely to impact on their ability to work with
older people in an empowering and sensitive manner. Furthermore,
interviews with people who had a diagnosis of dementia found that the
impact of negative cultural stereotypes of older people was compounded
by a diagnosis of dementia (Scholl and Sabat, 2008). This leaves people at

risk of negative self-stereotyping, which can be heightened if they access services such as memory clinics and day centres where people are in the more advanced stages of the illness. Scholl and Sabat (2008) argue that if ageing were viewed more positively the stigma pertaining to dementia would reduce. They suggest that carers can help the person with dementia by supporting them to gain a sense of internal control over their reducing memory, allocate the cared for areas of responsibility and encourage them to make decisions. We now move on to consider the impact of sexuality on identity.

Contextualising the Experience of Being Lesbian or Gay

Erben's Schema (1998) is again used to explore being a lesbian woman or a gay male as once more it allows us to reflect on the impact of societal context and cultural ideologies, and how these shape a sense of self informed by experience that through time can change and develop.

> When thinking of sexuality it is useful to recall its many dimensions. As part of an inner world of thoughts and feelings, sexuality fuels wants and desires. It holds a meaning that is intimate and personal. As an aspect of identify, sexuality imbues self-image and social relations and is a key feature of biography and life experience. At a structural level it serves as an axis upon which power relations are organized in society (Ward *et al.*, 2005: 49).

Historically lesbian and gay sexuality was understood as a perversion, and evidence of immorality and vice. The 1885 Criminal Law Amendment Act made sexual acts between men unlawful, while sexual acts between women were assumed to be non-existent (Turnball, 2002; Manthorpe and Price, 2005). For lesbian women and gay men born after the First World War their sexuality became defined as a disease, and secrecy and discretion in relationships were required. Persecution by the Nazis in the Second World War resulted in the death of 50,000 gay men in concentration camps.

The Gay Liberation Manifesto (1979) identified sources of external oppression including the family, school, church, media, language, employment, law, physical violence and psychiatry, culminating in self-oppression. Homosexuality was classified as psychiatric disease (and remained so until 1973) to be treated with psychotherapy or aversion therapy. Goffman (1963: 15) argued that even if the gay person receives psychiatric treatment and becomes "normal" they still assume the status of once being "blemished" (p.20). He went on to explain that the impact of the self-oppression and stigmatisation leads people to feel uncomfortable and ill at ease, vulnerable to victimisation, medical cures or faith treatments. Goffman discussed how there are opportunities to "pass" as heterosexual, but how those choosing to pass "must necessarily pay a great psychological price, a very high level of anxiety, in living a life that can be collapsed at any moment" (Goffman, 1963: 108). Thus "heteronormativity is transmitted by the norming practices and standards which privilege heterosexuality and heterosexual citizenship and relegate homosexuality to the ranks of 'other'" (Tolley and Ranzin, 2006: 79). This leads to the creation of dual identities. Clarke's (1996) research into the lives of lesbian Physical Education teachers demonstrates how the impact of "holding dual identities i.e. pseudo-heterosexual and lesbian has the potential to create great dissonance and personal turmoil" (p.196). The women used a range of strategies to disguise or deny their sexuality including the continued use of married status after divorce or the invention of a male partner. These types of 'passing' strategies were also articulated in research by Hunt *et al.*, (2007) commissioned by the Department of Health, where twenty-one health or social care workers commented on the general culture and direct harassment they had experienced. The eradication of homophobia was not a priority. There was an absence of equality policies and training courses pertaining to sexuality. An "out" lesbian or gay identity could adversely impact on career progression, and led some workers like the teachers to keep quiet about their sexuality. These attitudes were not confined to staff but included the patients:

> Before every shift starts – you have to hand over every patient – and if we do happen to have a gay person on the ward it's always mentioned. *Joan (District Nurse) North West*

> A patient explaining that she lived with another woman was described by a clerk as 'disgusting' in front of the podiatry manager - which he did not challenge. *Nancy (Community Specialist Podiatrist) North East*

These working environments, which are part of the education and welfare infrastructure, are emotionally unsafe cultures where to be or thought to be lesbian or gay can result in harsh punitive attitudes and behaviour. This does impact on the quality of the services provided. If staff discriminate against colleagues it is probable that:

> [W]e're discriminating against potential patients really because of these people (who) hold these views about gay colleagues it's going to transmit down to the patients eventually because when they are dealing with them

they're not maintaining professionalism. *Sharon (Pharmacist) North East*
(Hunt *et al.*, 2007: 7)

Discriminatory social attitudes are likely to make lesbian women and gay
men hesitant about how open they should be about their sexuality. The
Equality and Human Rights Commission (2009) has compiled research
findings including an online survey of 5,000 people. The purpose of the
research was to identify what needs to be done to deal with discrimination
and disadvantage experienced by lesbian, gay and bisexual people, and
what changes should be put in place within organisations to achieve the
changes required. The report acknowledges the citizenship rights that have
been achieved by lesbians, gay and bisexual people in the last five years:
civil partnerships; the entitlement to be considered as an adoptive parent;
right of succession as a housing tenant for same sex couples; protection
against discrimination in employment, facilities and services (Employment
Equality (Sexual Orientation) Regulations 2003), and the repeal of Section
28 of the Local Government Act (1988).

There is greater understanding now of human sexuality, and established
religion exerts less influence in matters of sexual preferences. Legislative
and policy changes have helped to bring about enlightenment. The civil
rights movement with the Stonewall Riots in 1969 was seen as a turning
point, where lesbians and gay men resisted against a culture of
intimidation that required secrecy about their sexuality (Gaine, 2010). As
more lesbian women and gay men have become open about their sexuality
in some social environments it ceases to be seen as exceptional. In 1987
when questioned if they thought being lesbian or a gay man was wrong
75% of people said yes; by 2008 this had reduced to 32% (British Social
Attitude Survey, 2008), but these welcome signs of progress need to be
viewed with caution in light of the high incidence of hate crime, with one
in eight lesbian women and gay men experiencing a crime or incident in
2007/08 (Dick, 2009). Ellison and Gunstone (2009) found the fear of
abuse or attack results in only 25% of lesbians and 29% of gay men
feeling safe in their own communities; as a consequence couples felt
harassed and unable to publicly express their affection for each other in
public such as holding their partner's hand walking down the street,
commonplace for heterosexual couples. The impact of homophobic
attitudes and behaviour found that 47% of lesbians and 42% of gay men
surveyed stated that they had experienced stress because of their sexuality
with 16% of lesbians and 9% of gay men reporting a current mental health
difficulty, in contrast to 6% of heterosexual women and 4% of heterosexual
men (Ellison and Gunstone, 2009).

In 2007 Stonewall surveyed 1,658 lesbian, gay and bisexual people in the UK about their views of entering politics. It established that most people believed they would face opposition from all political parties if they wished to be selected as a member of parliament, especially in terms of the Conservative Party (Hunt and Dick, 2007). There are few "out" politicians of any party, and this lack of access to political power means that issues pertaining to equality and citizenship rights for lesbian women, gay men and bisexual people have not been given sufficient political priority, compared with other marginalised groups.

It is unsurprising that many older lesbian and gay men have reduced expectations of social justice in contrast to younger people, as for much of their lives they will have experienced discrimination, oppression and heterosexism (Hughes, 2006). Hunt and Dick (2007) found that two in five lesbian women and gay men over the age of 50 years have low expectations of the Police if they reported a homophobic hate crime. Furthermore, one in fourteen lesbian women and gay men of all ages expects that their treatment will be worse if they are seeking health care.

The Equality and Human Rights Commission (EHRC) (2009) recommends that for equality to be achieved, organisations need to monitor sexual orientation, and should develop policies to support diversity. In addition, the delivery of services should be audited to check if equality standards are met, and staff training on sexuality should be provided. This is to eradicate bullying as reported by nearly 37% of lesbian women and gay men; 38% have felt frightened and 42% have suffered from low self-esteem. The EHRC recommend that specific research be undertaken to capture the experiences of older lesbian women and gay men, including those with dementia and their carers as:

> [H]istorical silencing of lesbians and gay men in social discourse and in mainstream research and health and social care provision is another key reason for the invisibility of this substantial group ... once a person has dementia, the diagnosis and its presumed personal and public consequences somehow become a person's chief defining characteristics. Other social identities are perceived as less important, or at least less pressing, and are thus extinguished in the observer's eye –a response, perhaps, to the persuasiveness and power of the stereotypes, stigma and discrimination that surround the condition (Price, 2008: 1340).

The impact of dementia on identity for the cared for and the carer is complex and difficult to manage. When this is coupled with being a lesbian woman or gay man this can be especially problematic, for the person's sexuality may be stigmatised, or may not be publicly acknowledged by health and social care services. Moore (2002: 26) writes that he had an "epiphany" on realising that support services for carers of people with dementia simply assumed heterosexuality for the person with dementia and the carer. A similar realisation came to Age Concern UK (2001) and in response they developed a resource pack for staff and volunteers, which acknowledged that many older lesbian women and gay men had led restricted public and social lives as a result of legislation, policies and attitudes which have criminalised, stigmatised and pathologised their sexuality. The aim is to provide information "[to] lead the way and to *throw open new doors"* (Smith and Calvert, 2001:12). The resource pack deconstructs "myths and misinterpretations" about lesbian women and gay men (Smith and Clavert, 2001: 8-12), which I will now review, paying particular attention to the needs of carers of people with dementia.

Myth 1: *"There aren't any round here":* this is an assumption based on the belief that lesbian women and gay men are easily identified by their appearance and behaviour. It feeds into stereotypes pertaining to "butch" lesbians and effeminate gay men. Furthermore, there can be assumptions that most lesbian women and gay men are primarily city dwellers, which is not the case. (For example, Age UK Berkshire has an active lesbian and gay older people's group.) This myth, that there are no lesbian women and gay men, will impact on the type of services commissioned, developed and provided. In addition older lesbian women and gay men are not routinely represented in advertisements and web sites where older people are often depicted as white, heterosexual, middle class and healthy, and therefore an explicit visual message is given as to whom services are targeted at (Ward *et al.,* 2005; Phillips and Marks, 2006).

Myth 2: *"They can look after their own":* underpinning this myth is a similar rationale to that used in the dearth of services for people from black and ethnic minority groups. This has led lesbian women and gay men to develop services to meet social care and health needs (Terence Higgins Trust, National Gay Funeral Helpline) and political campaigning organisations (Outrage!, Stonewall). For carers of someone with dementia specialist support and provision is likely to be necessary at some stage in the progress of the illness, and person centred care should be provided to both the person with dementia and the carer. The majority of research and policy documents pertaining to people with dementia and carers are heterosexualist and assume "traditional" family relationships.

Myth 3: *"We're open to everyone anyway":* again there are links to the justification given to not assessing and providing culturally appropriate services to people from black and minority ethnic communities. Some lesbian women and gay men living in care homes "may feel compelled to veil their sexuality" and this could well apply to their carers too (Ward *et al.,* 2005: p.53). Sexualised behaviour of residents can be seen as part of their dementia and "labelled as disinhibition" (p.58). Archibald (2006: 22) recounts the story of one woman who was thought to be lesbian by the staff in a care home. Her behaviour was assessed as sexualised and focused on female staff:

> … when Christine asked me to accompany her to her bedroom, I initially hesitated. I recorded my thoughts afterwards:

> Was there some sexual aspect as staff had said? But then I said, 'Come on' and just as quickly dismissed the sexual connotations. I did go with her, helped her undress and placed her on the commode. I spent 20 minutes with her talking to her about her family and past. As I was leaving she said 'Thank you for talking to me'.

Christine's needs, irrespective of having dementia and possibly being a lesbian woman, were simply a wish for positive interaction, and reminiscing.

Myth 4: *"No-one's ever asked for specific services for lesbian and gay men so obviously there is no need":* lesbian women and gay men are not a homogenous group and do not have one collective voice. Disputes can arise between friends and families, as illustrated by a friend of an older gay man:

> I was the close friend, 'significant other', referred to as the patient's 'carer' and 'advocate' by social services. The family, having had little contact with social services throughout the previous eight years he was in care, suddenly objected to my being in any way involved, receiving information or representing him as had happened over the previous nine years (Commission for Social Care Inspection, 2008b: 34-35).

In this case, the social services department agreed with the family and the friend was prevented from continued involvement. The man in care died before this was resolved. The friend took his case to the Local Government Ombudsman, who criticised the council's handling of the situation. Lipinska (2009: 78), in her role as a counsellor for people with dementia has witnessed the following regarding the partner of the person with dementia:

> In some cases, men and women whose same sex partner develops dementia
> may find themselves on the fringes of care, concern, services and legal
> provisions if there is not a civil union or clear 'Advanced Directives' to
> indicate who can make medical and care decisions if the partner is not
> 'next of kin'.

Underpinning family attitudes can be an assumption about the true value
and legitimacy of relationships, so a hierarchy of relationships can develop
(Finch, 1983) and lesbian and gay partnerships and friendships may not
figure in this.

Myth 5: *"We already have lesbian and gay clients – they just don't
flaunt it":* a familiar and popular critique of lesbian women and gay men
has been the 'flaunting' of sexuality. This is part of a view that suggests
that discretion is paramount and that being a lesbian woman or a gay man
is about sex, rather than comprising a social identity. Ironically
heterosexuality is pervasive in the media and arts and "flaunted" to market
merchandise and so on, unlike lesbian and gay sexuality that is rarely
featured. For example research that looked at the brochures of thirty older
people's care homes in Australia found that non-heterosexual identities
were excluded with the assumption that the "heterosexual experience is
the norm and the only legitimate worldview and reality" (Phillips and
Marks, 2006: 71). This explains the following observation:

> No other group of people is expected to leave a significant part of their
> identity outside the front door in order to feel comfortable gaining access
> to services. There is a big difference between 'flaunting' one's traits and
> habits, and feeling comfortable enough to be oneself (Smith and Clavert,
> 2001: 10).

Goffman (1963: 112) spoke of "living on a leash" unable to relax socially
with others, and referred to "disclosure etiquette" (p.124) where
information is shared on the basis that the reaction will not be hostile.
Only when lesbian women and gay men feel comfortable with their
sexuality do they reach a state of "above passing" (p.125).

Myth 6: *"They keep themselves to themselves":* this again resonates with
statements that can be made about particular ethnic or cultural groups, and
used to justify ethno-centric health and social care provision. Lesbian
women and gay men carers invariably have to "come out" to multiple
professionals, as a result of assumptions of "compulsory heterosexuality"
(Butler, 1993), as illustrated below:

Although we had taken out a power of attorney on behalf of each other (that is a legal document to ensure that either of us could administer the other's legal affairs in the event of serious illness), my early attempts to get help were marked by a failure, or even an unwillingness, by the various authorities to recognise my rights in dealing with David's condition, and accompanying that was a need to explain to everyone I had to deal with, what exactly the nature of my relationship was with him. In other words every new meeting became a demand to tell people that I was gay; so was HE; and we were PARTNERS. Can you imagine the stress and potential difficulties that situations might produce? (Newman, 2002, quoted by Turnball, 2001: 8)

This experience is unique to lesbian women and gay men and produces additional stressors that are on-going aspects of care giving not one off events (Harrison, 2006; Phillips and Marks, 2006; Zarit and Zarit, 2008), that are not found in heterosexual relationships. Moore (2002) established a telephone support group for five lesbian women and two gay male carers who were supporting partners with dementia in rural North Carolina in the USA. The group was set up because services for carers were being "created within a heterosexual framework in which older lesbians and gay men are placed in a position of either denying or concealing their sexual identity" (Moore, 2002: 26). The Alzheimer's Society withdrew its support due to "concerns about professional appearance, propriety, and fund raising" (p.27). The carers spoke of their isolation when attending support groups with other carers who identified as heterosexual:

You can't imagine how I felt [when they] started to introducing themselves. Since most were either married or indicated they were there because either their mother or dad had Alzheimer's, I recognized I was different. I just froze. Should I tell them about my partner? Should I just say I have a friend and want more information about the disease? ... All I knew was how we have tried to be discreet and quiet about our private lives all these years (Moore, 2002: 29).

When the nature of their relationship became known, this could result in health staff looking quizzical and asking questions in a hesitant manner. One carer described being older and lesbian as a frightening experience:

"We were the side show," she added, recalling several particular situations. After admission, the caregiver spoke to the patient's primary nurse case manager about staying overnight since the patient sometimes became more agitated and confused at night. The nurse responded condescendingly, "Honey, you know we can only allow a relative to stay with the patient. We know how to take care of your older friend." The next morning the same caregiver overheard the nursing students chuckling in the hallway,

"In this room we have a pair of old gray lesbians." Their attitude was that older lesbians shouldn't be affectionate with each other, as if "after 50, passion, caring, and tenderness dry up." She noted that being an older lesbian is frightening because "physicians and nurses see us differently" (Moore, 2002: 31).

This is a small scale piece of research, but illustrates the change required by some organisations before it is understood that services need to "come out" as lesbian and gay friendly rather than expecting older people to "out" themselves. The impact of the group on the carers was positive as they reported feeling less isolated and confirmed their commitment to support their partner at home as long as possible. We will now consider how carers are defined by social policy and look at how caring has been theorised, which leads us into the societal context of caring (Erben, 1998).

CHAPTER TWO

THE CONCEPT OF CARING

Introduction

This chapter will consider how the concept of being a carer has developed. This will be achieved by examining evolving social policy that has led to the social inclusion rather than exclusion of disabled people. The role of informal carers has been paramount to achieve this policy objective. We will also consider how caring has been theorised, which influences the practice of social care and health care practitioners and the development of services.

Developments in Social Policy

Social policy has shifted from care provided in institutions through workhouses in the 19th century, to individualised care with the personalisation of care services in the 21st century (Gardner, 2011). The notion of family obligation, and expectations by successive governments that families should continue to care so the concept of family is not undermined, have been consistent factors in social policy, for example, "social care is not solely the responsibility of the state" (Department of Health, 2010b). An emphasis on family obligation is a powerful economic driver, so that costs are not all met by the state, but by individuals and families too.

The cultural legacy of institutional care remains a factor for many older people as a result of their memories of subnormality hospitals (sic) and mental asylums (sic). Although the old institutions are largely gone, inpatient care is provided in the NHS, private and third sector care homes. The average number of beds in a private sector care home in the UK is 40 for older people (Innes, 2009). According to government figures, one-third of people with dementia live in care homes, and at least two-thirds of all people living in care homes have a form of dementia (Department of Health, 2009). Goffman (1961: 17) defined total institutions as:

A basic social arrangement in modern society is that the individual tends to sleep, play, and work in different areas, with different co-participants, under different authorities, and without an overall rational plan. The central feature of total institutions can be described as a breakdown of the barriers ordinarily separating these three spheres of life.

Goffman's characterisation of an institution could be used to describe the cultural regimes in many care homes where older people are often passive, bored and socially isolated. This type of culture has been identified as a priority for improvement, as has the need for greater social interaction given that "the typical person in a care home spent just two minutes interacting with staff or other residents over a six-hour period of observation (excluding time spent on care tasks)" (Department of Health 2009: 58).

This type of care is colloquially known as "warehousing" where only people's basic physical needs are met. It is well established that high quality dementia care should focus on all aspects of the person's needs through an understanding of their biography, by engaging with the carer, family and friends. Positive interactions are fundamental to the well-being of people with dementia. Bryden (2005: 127), who has early onset dementia, advises:

How you relate to us has a big impact on the course of the disease. You can restore our personhood, and give us a sense of being needed and valued. There is a Zulu saying that is very true, 'A person is a person through others'. Give us reassurance, hugs, support, a meaning in life. Value us for what we can still do and be, and make sure we retain social networks.

One of the positive aspects of community care services, which support people to remain within their own homes, has been the acknowledgement that people who use services should be central to the process. For carers there has been an explicit recognition of their role, which subsequently led to legislation providing them with entitlements to financial and practical support. Social policy recognises that people should not be fitted into existing provision, although the resources to develop innovative and person centred services were not sufficient (Gorman and Postle, 2003). Eligibility criteria to access an assessment for services has become increasingly restrictive, so that only people with the highest level of need are assessed for services, and services provided by Local Authorities are means-tested. In 2010 HM Government published research based on the views of 4,000 carers, about the priorities for service delivery. It found that insufficient assistance was provided, many carers were not routinely offered a carer's assessment, and there was a shortage of high quality respite care or domiciliary care (Gardner, 2009; HM Government, 2010).

Carers' experience of hospital provision does not fare any better, although people with dementia aged over 65 years occupy 25% of hospitals beds at any one time. Evidence provided by 2,000 carers (Lakey, 2009) showed that 54% said that a stay in hospital for the person with dementia created more confusion and dependency, and 47% said that the person's general health declined. It was found that 77% of carers were dissatisfied with the overall quality of care provided for the person with dementia in hospital. They complained of nursing staff having little understanding of the impact of dementia; a lack of person centred care; limited social interaction; not being supported to eat or drink; both the person with dementia and the carer being excluded from decision making, and overall the person with dementia not being treated with dignity and respect. It is evident that the closure of institutions and the implementation of care in the community have not led to the development of high quality services for older people and in particular people with dementia (Means et al., 2008). There is a mismatch between social policy and the lived experience of people requiring support in the community. This was highlighted by Rolph et al. (2005: 21) in their research tracking the lives of people with learning disabilities and their families from 1920 to 2001: "Most accounts of social policy, however, have tended to focus on the 'high politics' of policy evolution, with much less known about implementation at local level, including the role played by service users, families and communities". They suggest that there is an "official history" (p.19) that implies services are continually improving through an enlightened understanding of the needs of disabled people and carers, which is evidenced by social policy, legislation and records. In reality the experience of disabled people and carers shows that social inclusion and person centred service provision have not been realised.

Doherty et al. (2009: 503) mapped the experience of two people with dementia through health and social care services observing that:

> the illness journey is a new experience through unchartered territory – there is no A-Z or road atlas ... From diagnosis, through treatment and to the end of life, the path is often not easy, and may be seen as a journey of epic proportions by those facing it

They found services fragmented and uncoordinated and made the following recommendations: the person with dementia should be provided with a key worker to ensure on-going support. Relevant information including obtaining a Power of Attorney should be given. Direct payments should always be offered, so the person with dementia and carer can arrange services. Night services should be provided and flexible transport to day care centres that fit with carers' work patterns. Services should be developed that meet the needs of people from black and minority ethnic communities. Care in the community has now developed into the concept of personalisation in the assessment, provision and funding of services. A contextual factor is demography, as people are living longer, and with increasing age more demands are made on health and social care services (Department of Health, 2010b). By 2022, 20% of the population in England will be over 65 and the government acknowledge that while "the Community Care legislation of the 1990s was well intentioned, it has led to a system which can be over complex and too often fails to respond to people's needs and expectations" (Department of Health, 2008b; Gardner, 2009).

The aim of personalisation is the development of service provision that meets individual needs through self-assessment and the increased use of direct payments and individual budgets, so that people can purchase their own services (Department of Health, 2008b). There are significant benefits to this approach, especially where services are not meeting identified need, as already highlighted for people with dementia, but also in terms of marginalised groups such as lesbian women and gay men, and people from black and ethnic minority communities. The success of this approach will require sufficient government funding. The concept of the "big society" developed by the Coalition Government suggests increased responsibility for the provision of social care services will fall to families and communities. "We can transform care, not by looking upwards to the state, but outwards to open communities – by empowering individuals and unlocking the power and creativity of neighbourhoods" (Department of Health, 2010b: 9). This ambitious aim does require sufficient state funding. The government views local authorities as the engine to develop the big society and the role of national government is "to facilitate, assure and support" (Department of Health, 2010b: 32); however this shift in responsibility emerges during a period of severe reductions in government funding to local authorities.

Conceptualising Carers

The concept of "carer" as applied to care provided by family and friends is a recent one, and is socially constructed, as a term that encapsulates people's experiences and is used in policy (Bytheway and Johnston, 1998). The Carers National Association was established in 1986, which provided a pressure group that sought to improve the financial, social and emotional support provided to carers. The assumption was that most carers were women and that caring was a one-to-one relationship rather than involving other family members and friends (Finch *et al.*, 1983). The General Household Survey (1985) challenged these cultural assumptions by reporting that 40% of carers were male, although there was some dispute about the figure as men may have defined themselves as carers more readily than women when they had to undertake domestic tasks not previously their responsibility.

There were debates between feminists regarding women and care. Some argued that care in the community required women to support older and disabled people, who were conceptualized as a burden. For example, Finch (1984) and Dalley (1987) advocated the use of residential care for disabled people, to ensure that women were not required to be unpaid carers, and excluded from the labour market. This was subjected to a robust critique led by the disabled feminist Morris (1991) who argued that very often disabled and older people were themselves carers, that disabled people wanted to be independent and self sufficient. For this reason care in the family may not be the preferred option for many people in old age, although notions of responsibility are linked with kinship (Letherby, 2002). Difficulties were, and still are caused by social environments and government policy which excluded and marginalised disabled and older people. Implicit in these views was an "us and them" perspective which did not reflect that these able bodied women may themselves become disabled as they grew older, and that many of the cared for were women (Morris, 1991: 154). The relationship between the cared for and carer can be blurred with a mutual dependency, and needs to be re-conceptualised further:

> We may also want to expand our definition of caring for to encompass not just physical tasks but also the emotional part of caring for relationships. Research carried out by disabled feminists would, therefore, focus not so much on *carers* as on *caring* (Morris, 1991: 167).

Care is often seen as a one to one relationship when it is more appropriate to think of a "caring system". Research in South Wales found that care is often provided by a range of people rather than a single carer, and that gender was less important than issues of capacity and other commitments; for example people without paid employment and who did not have other caring commitments tend to provide more care (Bytheway *et al.,* 1998). There can be an "hierarchy of care" in terms of expectations of caring responsibilities, with the partner or relative living in the same house being seen as the main carer, followed by daughter, then daughter-in-law, son, other relative and finally non-relative. These expectations become disrupted in families where relatives are not all living in the UK, or if the family members do not live nearby (Stalker, 2003).This links to Finch's (1984) notion of family obligations which are implicit understandings within families about who is responsible for the bulk of caring with more traditionally expected of women than men.

Most research regarding the experience of caring has consisted of small scale studies often confirming each other (Stalker, 2003).The dominant models for interpreting caring have been that of caring as experienced in the same way by everyone, or that of caring as a burden; however, caring needs to be understood in the context of the relationship between the cared for and the carer (Twigg and Atkin, 1994). In the case of dementia it is essential to recognise that this is especially challenging because the cognitive abilities of the person being cared for are in decline, creating particular stress for the carer as dependency on them increases.

Burton (2006), in research using a focus group and interviews with fourteen carers, emphasises that the relationship between the cared for and carer is paramount in understanding the experience of caring, and maintains that not all carers experience a sense of burden. Relationships can be ones of interdependency and mutual reward. Burton's carers identified their difficulties as lack of information about health conditions: limited understanding of the roles of health and social care professionals, and an absence of emotional and practical help. In Switzerland, Perren *et al.* (2006) used a random controlled study with carers and found that carers reported that they benefited from support and information provided through structured sessions, in contrast to those carers who were not provided with this service.

Thomas (2010: 131) writes of her "rage" about the care that her mother received, and her own lack of understanding about her mother's health needs, or how to effectively advocate for her in the nursing home where she was placed:

> Even though it was written in her notes that she was to be washed and toileted by women only, my mum – who wouldn't enter a lavatory in her own house if there was anyone there to observe her doing so – was handled by men daily. I remember one particular example. Some relatives were visiting from America and Mum had been dressed in a beautiful, expensive frock, which before she went into hospital she had been keeping for a special occasion. She was so nervous that she asked to go to the toilet, but instead of wheeling her into the one opposite, the two male carers pushed a commode into her room just as her visitors arrived. We waited outside until they brought out the uncovered receptacle and told us to go in. I rushed to open the window as we tried not to retch. Mum was deeply humiliated, mortified, the visit was ruined...

> Poor Mum. She slipped further and further away from me, from reality. 'This place is closing down next week,' she'd tell me. 'I could do with some runner beans. I've got a nice leg of pork to cook lunch for Beryl'. Why did no one ever tell me that I shouldn't have corrected her when she said irrational things? Even a leaflet would have helped. I know now that I should have behaved as if she were being sensible. 'Am I talking rubbish *again*?' she'd ask. I know it made her not want to speak (Thomas, 2010: 132 -134).

This deeply distressing account illustrates the importance of carers being informed and educated about dementia, as well as what to do if services are degrading and poor in quality. The development of personalisation as the future direction of health and social care services is underpinned by person centred care practices that recognise the interaction and interdependency between the person with dementia and other people. These are of course universal human needs (Department of Health, 2010c). Nolan *et al.,* (2001) have developed the concept of relationship-centred care, which highlights the importance of positive relationships for the person with dementia and the carer. This can be linked back to caring as a system which may involve informal carers such as family and friends as well as formal (paid) carers. This approach resonates with "whole-family approaches" (Bytheway *et al.,* 1998; Department of Health, 2010c:7).

Hellström *et al.,* (2007) undertook research that did not just take account of the carers' views but also those of the person with dementia and in so doing sought to avoid their marginalisation from the research. Twenty couples were interviewed over five years in Sweden. The findings provide a challenge to the stress/burden model of care giving, and offer a

Figure 2-1: Couplehood in Dementia

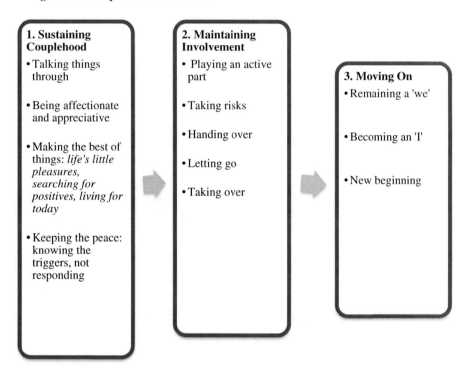

1. Sustaining Couplehood

- Talking things through

- Being affectionate and appreciative

- Making the best of things: *life's little pleasures, searching for positives, living for today*

- Keeping the peace: knowing the triggers, not responding

2. Maintaining Involvement

- Playing an active part

- Taking risks

- Handing over

- Letting go

- Taking over

3. Moving On

- Remaining a 'we'

- Becoming an 'I'

- New beginning

Time

(Adapted from Hellstöm, *et al.,* 2007: 390)

more optimistic analysis of how dementia is managed on a daily basis. The research focused on how couples used a range of strategies to live positively. There are three phrases to the model, which does not necessarily proceed within a clear time frame. This is set out in figure 2.1. Men as well as women carers tried to sustain the relationship with the person with dementia. Hellström *et al.* made a recommendation that service providers adopt a relationship-centred approach so that partnerships could be better supported and maintained. The sexuality of the couples is not discussed in the research, but the tone of the research suggests that the couples were in the main heterosexual and married. They found that most of the couples in their sample had positive relationships, but where this was not the case if more had been known by the professionals, any difficulties would have become apparent earlier and alternative care could have been provided. The model does emphasise how people sought to live companionably together in spite of the dementia.

This process was not always consistent, but the research found that this was overall an observable pattern within relationships.

Chung *et al.* (2008) developed a model that also follows the trajectory of the illness. It is based on the data following interviews with thirty carers. They understood their relationship with the person with dementia through a continuum of activity patterns, as the dementia progressed shared activities between the carer and cared for became progressively more difficult. The carers' "sense of self through their past relationship with the relative faded in front of their eyes, removing a life support and making the carers feel even more isolated" (Chung *et al.* (2008: 377). The activity patterns of the person with dementia went through five stages where it became increasingly difficult for the carer and cared for to do things together on an equal basis. This had an emotional impact on the carer and at each stage they formulated different strategies to cope. The activity patterns are as follows:

Figure 2-2: Activity Patterns Dementia

Chung *et al.* (2008) concluded that the activity continuum was useful for health and social care practitioners as it gave them insight into the carers' experience, so they could offer appropriate support to carers at different stages of the continuum. These models have considered the stages in which caring changes for both the person with dementia and the carer. We will now theorise the process of caring in terms of the impact on the carer and how this fits with service delivery to the cared for.

Theorising Caring

Twigg and Atkin (1994) have identified three approaches to caring: balancing/boundary setting, engulfment mode and symbiotic mode. Balancing/boundary setting mode is where caring is viewed as a job, in contrast to the engulfment mode that is characterised by the person's self identity being defined as a carer where "their emotional identification with the cared for person was often so close that they found it difficult to separate themselves from the cared for person's pain and suffering", and is more prevalent with women than men (Twigg and Atkin, 1994: 122). It entails an inability for carers to articulate their own needs; difficulty in accepting services and an overwhelming sense of responsibility for the cared for person. This contrasts with the "symbiotic mode" (p.125) where there are positive mutual benefits for both the carer and the cared for. In these circumstances carers are able to accept services for the cared for person, but services for themselves are seen as unnecessary, as they derive benefits from their role, although for carers of people with dementia it is highly improbable they will be able to continue to care without support for the duration of the illness.

Tanner and Harris (2008) have developed four models that describe the identity and role of carers that impact on how health and social care professionals interface with carers, which in turn will affect the carers' sense of self-identity. I have presented this as a diagram (figure 2.4) to demonstrate that the models are not fixed, but can move and change over time. If this is related to a carer of a person with dementia this course may be followed as the illness progresses.

Figure 2-3: Approaches to Caring

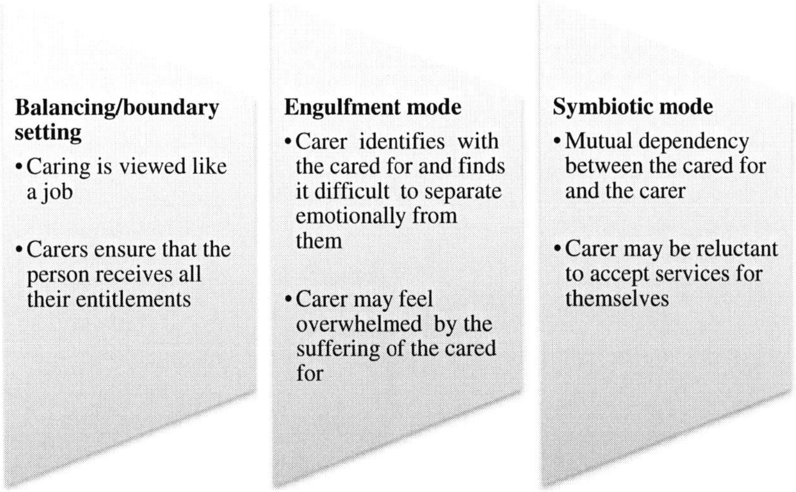

Balancing/boundary setting
• Caring is viewed like a job
• Carers ensure that the person receives all their entitlements
Engulfment mode
• Carer identifies with the cared for and finds it difficult to separate emotionally from them
• Carer may feel overwhelmed by the suffering of the cared for
Symbiotic mode
• Mutual dependency between the cared for and the carer
• Carer may be reluctant to accept services for themselves

(Adapted from Twigg and Atkin, 1994)

Figure 2-4: Models of Carers of People with Dementia

Carer as Resource
Carer as Co-worker
Carer as Co-client
Superseded Carer

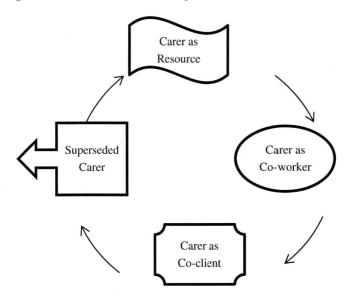

Adapted from Tanner and Harris (2008:178)

These models are found within legislation and policy (Phillips e*t al.*, 2006). The NHS and Community Care Act 1990 envisaged carers as providing services at no cost to the health and welfare system; when legislation developed that saw carers as citizens the concept of carer as co-worker developed (Department of Health, 2010c). In social policy terms this has moved through into carer as co-client with an acknowledgment of their needs, and finally to carer as superseded, where carers give up the role of carer. These stages and processes are complex and can be experienced as highly emotional and distressing for carers. This model can be linked to Hellstöm *et al.'s* (2007) framework of "couple-hood" in dementia where the impact of illness changes the nature of the relationship. We will now turn to consider the process of researching the experiences of carers, prior to immersing ourselves in their stories.

CHAPTER THREE

REFLECTIONS ON THE RESEARCH PROCESS

Introduction

This chapter provides my rationale for the qualitative research approach and biographical method that I used when I interviewed carers of people with dementia. The process that I adopted is explained together with my reflections on the interviewing method as a research instrument, and my role as the researcher in the process. This is followed by a critical overview of the limitations and strengths of the research methodology. Ethical issues are explored in the context of the overall process and my responsibilities as the researcher.

Research Approach

The research method and approach clearly needed to be appropriate to understand the experience of caring and what enables carers to continue to care for the person with dementia as the illness progresses and to identify health and social care practice that was helpful, and supportive with the purpose of utilising this knowledge in health and social care education. Research should have relevance, validity and be feasible to undertake (Denscombe, 1998). The prevalence of dementia is increasing due to an ageing population (Department of Health, 2009). The economic significance of carers supporting disabled people is £87 billion per annum, an average of £15,260 per carer (CarersUK cited by Galpin and Bates, 2009). As such the research had relevance due not only to the economic importance of carers, but the positive impact of continuing social relationships for people with dementia (Kitwood, 1997).

Throughout the course of the research I sought to implement criteria to assess validity developed by Etheringdon (2004), who states that the researcher's reflexivity should be apparent by demonstrating an awareness of how the researcher impacted on the research process, and conversely how the process affected them. The social, cultural and political context in which people live: "the variety of communities they inhabit (and which inhabit them)" and their relative power or powerlessness needs to be acknowledged with a recognition that the outcomes of research can achieve changes to power (Griffiths, 1998: 95). Moreover research should give voice to a range of different perspectives with opportunities for creativity in their expression, so that new learning and knowledge are obtained. Griffiths (1998: 129) argues research should achieve "better knowledge", and aim to enhance social justice by being underpinned by a series of ethical principles. She defines social justice as "what is good for common interest, where that is taken to include the good of each and the good of all, in an acknowledgement that one depends on the other" (p.95). One of the aims of my research was to better understand the experience of caring so this could inform health and social care practice.

The research was feasible as I found six carers who were prepared to be interviewed; of these two identified as lesbian women and one as a gay man. Being lesbian or gay was a criterion for half of the participants, as the views of lesbian women and gay male carers are rarely prominent in the research literature (Cass *et al.*, 2008). The study was located within the context of social work research that:

> aims not only to support practice but also to transform it. Social work with its ethical imperative towards challenging social injustice requires social work researchers to examine both the socially excluded and the powerful elites who decide upon their social exclusion (McLaughlin, 2007:13).

The research method needed to capture carers' stories in a way that could change public perceptions by providing a more authentic account of how carers viewed their experience of caring for someone with dementia, and what helps in terms of health and social care practice. As Steedman (1986:6) states: "Personal interpretations of past time – the stories people tell themselves in order to explain how they got to the place they currently inhabit – are often in deep and ambiguous conflict with the official interpretative devices of a culture".

Steedman was writing about how working-class lives had been defined by male historians, who wrote only about the lives of men, and which bore no relationship to the reality of her working-class mother. In a similar way there are also common cultural assumptions about carers held by health and social care staff, for example, that the majority of carers are women, that care is based on family obligation and all care is burdensome (Dalley, 1987). In fact one in eight people are carers - six million people in the UK

- of whom 42% are men and 58% are women (CarersUK cited by Galpin and Bates, 2009). Although being a carer can be stressful and difficult, carers do report satisfaction that relates to their personal relationship with the cared for (Nolan *et al.,* 2001).

The selection of a research method is based on the aims and objectives of the research and ethical implications for the research participants. In my view a positivist scientific approach would have been inappropriate as the research was attempting to understand experience rather than prove anything. "Quantitative research aims to show you what is happening. Qualitative research on the other hand, sets out to tell you why it is happening" (Moore, 2000:121). The idea that research can be unbiased, "scientific" and that distortion can be eliminated with the findings being reliable and valid is open to challenge (Briggs, 2003). For example the outcome of interviews may reflect more about the researcher than the interviewee. Letherby (2004) reminds us that research methods should fit the aims and objectives of the research, and additionally how the method is used will impact on the knowledge gained: "what we do affects what we get: the relationship between process and product / doing and knowing" (p.183). There may be an imbalance of power in so far as the researcher has formulated the questions asked and the probes that are used to extract more information. Furthermore there may be differences in social class, gender, ethnic origin, as well as theoretical perspectives between the interviewee and researcher. The latter might be seeking to confirm views already held. These issues are especially problematic when the research participants do not have access to the means by which stereotypes can be challenged, as only the voices of the powerful are heard. "When interviews provide the nation-state and its institutions with representations of marginalized populations, the possibilities for constructing a 'minority voice' that confirms the hegemonic status quo is thus acute" (Briggs, 2003: 243).

As the researcher I needed to be reflective, open minded with a willingness to learn and conscious of my own values (McLaughlin, 2007). This perspective is congruent with the principles of anti-oppressive practice which are entrenched in social work's values (Braye and Preston-Shoot, 1995). There is a growing awareness about the effective engagement of users and carers in the research process, which is being: '"internalized" by researchers informing their way of thinking' (Morgan and Harris, 2005). Beresford (2005: 8) describes the "democratic approach" in research, as the commitment to a shift of power and control towards those that access social care services and this is the approach that I sought to follow through my choice of the kind of interview I would conduct. Leamy and Clough (2006) found this approach had positive benefits for older people, as it led to increased political awareness, a sense of optimism about the ability to effect change and enjoyment at working collaboratively with other people. A similar situation was reflected in my study whereby the carers were active in the interviews, and narrated their story using the interview schedule loosely. They were not viewed by me as objects of data, or controlled in the process (Letherby, 2004; McLaughlin, 2007).

Simons (2009) suggests that the study of the individual is important, as it demonstrates how policies and procedures are implemented and their impact. For example only one of the carers had definitely been offered a carer's assessment, one other carer suspected that they might have been offered one, but could not confirm this. This has been a legal entitlement since 1995 but for these carers this aspect of government legislation and policy was not being implemented. Research that engages with the individual gives access to the "lived experience" (p.75) of the person and offers "insight into the idiosyncratic nature of particular events and experience that cannot be captured by other means. Its value lies in enabling us to understand, how a study of the particular yields universal understanding" (Simons, 2009: 77). The carers' stories provided a rich commentary about the reality of being a carer to someone with dementia. They highlighted health and social practice that were at times in variance with social policy intentions.

Research Design

Research needs to have a design and process developed so it can achieve the researcher's aims and objectives. Punch (2000: 23) suggests that a "hierarchy of concepts" be developed to guide the research. I have adapted this into a framework through which I sought to move the research from general aims to specific areas of investigation that addressed what enabled the carers to continue to care, and their experience of health and social care services. The research framework was developed into an interview schedule that sought basic details about the carer and the cared for as well as a self-classification of ethnic origin, gender, sexual orientation and age. My aim was to produce a research framework that would shift:

> the researcher from 'knowledge-privileged investigator' to a reflective position of passive participant/audience member in the storytelling process. The interviewer as writer/storyteller then emerges later in the process

through her/his retelling of the story as a weaver of tales, a collage-maker
or a narrator of narrations (Jones, 2002: 2).

In terms of the researcher being a "weaver of tales" it was necessary to
consider whose stories I wanted to capture, and how I could ensure that the
carers felt comfortable meeting with me. I offered the carers a choice of
where we met. They all invited me to their homes. I realised that it was
important for both the carers' comfort and convenience that the interviews
took place in a location of their choosing. None of the carers had the
person with dementia living with them, but if they had I would have asked
that we met when the cared for was not present so they were not
marginalised and objectified by the interview.

Etherington (2004: 77) starts her interviews by asking: "Where does your
story begin?" which was an approach I did not adopt but in hindsight
would be an effective first question, as it puts the research participant at
the centre of interview. My research practice was informed by "feminist
ways of working, where there is a focus on collaboration and dismantling
hierarchies" (Ramsay & Letherby, 2006: 27). Hence I chose not to take
notes, but taped the interviews with the participants' consent. I wanted to
be able to maintain eye contact, and I felt that it may impede their flow of
speech if I was writing. Moreover, I needed to be able to observe the
carers' facial expressions and body movements throughout the course of
the interviews as, while recognising that non-verbal communication is
"culture specific", I was also aware that where a "statement is made
verbally which is contradicted by body language, it is generally the body
language which is given credence" (Thompson, 2003: 100). I was
particularly alert to signs of distress, and wanted to convey an empathetic
response, as I knew that "the process of dementia is also the story of a
tragic inadequacy in our culture, our economy, our traditional views about
gender, our medical system and our general way of life" (Kitwood,1997:
41). I wanted the carers to know that I was authentic and non-judgemental
towards them in my wish to hear about their experiences (Egan, 2010).
The process of the interviews is explored in more detail later in the
chapter.

Selection of Carers

Liamputtong (2007: 27) developed the concept of the "sensitive
researcher" where the subjects of research are people who are socially
marginalised, and often disempowered by cultural and interpersonal
attitudes towards them. By explicitly ensuring that half the carers defined

themselves as lesbian women or gay men this situation was in part avoided as it enabled their views to be heard, as much of the research assumes that carers are heterosexual. A leaflet I developed about the research was distributed to lesbian and gay organisations and through informal networks and contacts. Snowballing took place and carers started to contact me. Another criterion was that at least half the carers had been caring in the last five years, as I wished to assess the impact of recent legislation and policy. The carers were all actively involved in the lives of the person with dementia, or had been if they had died.

I was mindful that for all carers it was likely that questions developed through the Users' and Carers' Involvement Movement (Beresford, 2005) were likely to figure in their decision about whether to be involved in the research. The five questions developed by Crepaz-Keay (2006), who is active in the Involvement Movement, were adapted for this research:

- What is the point of being involved in the research?

- Who should be involved? (Am I the best person to do this?)

- What is entailed? (Is this a postal questionnaire, telephone conversation or a face to face interview?)

- What can the research achieve? (Is it worth doing?)

- Is it safe? (Is this research ethical and confidential?)

The carers approached me usually by email, which was often followed by a telephone conversation where the above questions could be explored. An interview schedule containing information about the research project was sent, and this set down the questions that I would ask. These discussions and exchanges of information were essential in enabling the carers to have an accurate sense of the purpose of the research, and an understanding of what it could achieve.

Biographical Research Method

A biographical research method was used, that was limited in focus to the period of time that the participants had been carers. Biographical research uses narratives in the way in which people describe and explain their lives. It requires:

a critical scrutiny of the self. Indeed, those who protect the self from scrutiny could be considered self-satisfied and arrogant in presuming that their presence and relations with others are unproblematic. Auto/biography, then, enables us to locate the contextual within the personal (Ramsay and Letherby, 2006: 29).

Through the carers' stories patterns and themes emerge which are culturally and time specific (Erben, 1998; Plummer, 2001). It provides general information about the culture and society in which the person lives, as well as recording the individual's experiences. Bingley *et al.* (2008: 654) explain the nature of storytelling noting that stories appear:

> to be sparked by experiences of a 'breach' or 'disruption', however minor, in our usual patterns of life. Stories, therefore, gain a particular relevance at times of life transition or change, seemingly as a way of 'sense-making' or attempting to re-shape and manage the shifting grounds of our lives.

The diagnosis and onset of dementia are life-changing events, as described by Bingley, not just for the person concerned but for partners, family and friends. The progressive impact of dementia is often described by carers as losing the person they once knew. For example,

> When David's behaviour started to show signs of a fundamental change, it didn't take long before that well-established pattern of our lives began to fall apart. We had built a wall around our relationship which made us feel that it was easy being a gay couple and we truly believed that that was how it was going to be ... The onset of David's dementia, however, turned everything upside down ... having no real knowledge of the condition, my first reaction to his changed behaviour was to feel that he had decided that the relationship was over, and consequently I left him (Newman, 2010: 146).

Newman's account vividly and movingly describes how his partner's sexual behaviour with other men became more extreme and how emotionally damaged he felt by this. Denzin (1989: 70) stresses the importance of turning points or "epiphanies: interactional moments and experiences which leave marks on people's lives". These, he notes, "are often moments of crisis. In Newman's account there is the turning point of his partner's behaviour followed by the "epiphany" of understanding, when he realises the impact of dementia on David's behaviour. Newman went on to care for David and established the Lesbian, Gay, Bisexual and Transgendered (LGBT) Group at the Alzheimer's Society.

Epiphanies offer a valuable method or concept in understanding aspects of the carers' stories. The carers chose to remain involved with the person with dementia, which prevented the person becoming socially isolated, which often occurs (Commission for Social Care Inspection, 2008a). Some of the carers were able to state that they had consciously made this decision, which was an epiphany or turning point for them. They recognised the changes that would take place in their relationship to the person, which involved an increased dependency on them. Denzin (1989) defines four different types of epiphanies, which I have illustrated through their application to the stories of the carers I interviewed. The first is a *major event* which impacts on every aspect of the person's life such as the onset of dementia. Another epiphany is a *representative act* when a crisis occurs. A *minor event* epiphany is an occurrence that encapsulates a significant issue in the person's life which in itself does not seem important, but represents a defining moment in time - *reliving the event* is remembering an incident with the associated emotional impact.

One of the strengths of the biographical method is that it allows complexities to be studied in depth and understood. The social and cultural context of people's lives underpins their stories. Plummer (2001) highlights the importance of memory and identifies different types of memory, such as collective memories of particular experiences, that groups of people have had who have a shared identity, such as being a lesbian woman or gay man. Plummer develops the concept of "transformative remembering" (p.237) - an active process that enables memories to be shaped by increased self-knowledge. I wanted the carers to benefit from their participation in the study and the feedback that I received from some of the carers was that it had been helpful to tell their stories, as reflecting back had developed their sense of self, indeed the more the carers spoke so their confidence and understanding appeared to increase. Moon's (1999:157) earlier research identified the outcomes of reflection as self-development, empowerment and emancipation where "transformative learning" can take place through a critical self-appraisal, and evaluation of social and political contexts. Such outcomes were evident for some of my research participants.

I learnt from the research process too and reflecting back on the experience I concur with Etherington's (2004: 78) rationale for the use of this research approach:

> my intentions in gathering data in this way is that, in telling their stories,
> participants (and researchers) may also gain something for themselves. It

seems to me the very best possible outcome of research is that it provides an opportunity for growth and learning for both the researcher and researched as well as the wider community.

Etherington gives an example of the impact of being a researcher. One of her students, who was training to be a counsellor and therefore had to receive counselling herself as part of the course, said being a researcher increased her autonomy, self-awareness, reflexivity and problem solving skills more than receiving counselling. She developed criticality through developing connections in the analysis of the data and ultimately making sense of her research findings. These comments find resonance in my own experience of hearing the carers' stories, as a researcher rather than in my previous professional role of social worker, as in the latter role I would have felt compelled to do *something* rather than "valuing narrative ways of knowing" that allowed me to simply listen to the "lived experiences" of the carers (Etherington, 2004: 74).

For research to have credibility it needs to be accurate in reflecting the situation; relevant, timely, useful and trustworthy. It becomes "intrinsically qualitative" when "subjectivity, emotionality and feeling" are stressed (Simons, 2009:129). On the other hand Plummer (2001: 234) views "narrative memory" as consisting of stories that we chose to remember, and of course "memory may reify the life into something it is not". Life stories are constructed by the teller, so there may be limited historical objective truth. This contrasts with positivist research that is assessed against the criteria of reliability, validity, objectivity and whether it can be replicated. However, the purpose of the research was to understand the *experience* of the carers as they understood it themselves, with the recognition that "memory is no simple 'psychological faculty' from within – it is shaped through and through by setting, society and culture" (Plummer, 2001: 236). I ensured that I knew when the carer had been caring and for how long, as this enabled me to cross-reference their experiences of services within a legislative and policy context for themselves as carers, as well as the person with dementia. As already stated, a criterion for the sample was that a proportion of the carers had been caring in the last five years since the implementation of key policy and legislation, which may have impacted on their experience (Mental Capacity Act 2005; Department of Health, 2008a, 2009).

Interpretation of the Carers' Stories

In hearing the carers' stories I adopted an interpretive approach reflecting my desire to understand the purpose and the context of the carers' stories. Plummer (2001: 233) makes the point that: "Life story work involves recollecting, remembering, re-discovery, along with the active process of memorializing and constructing history" so from a sociological perspective it is not just the unique nature of individual lives but their social context (Roberts, 2002).

Narrative is organised around plots, characters, themes and genres. Stories personalise people's experiences, and provide access to people's thoughts and feelings. They are coherent through being placed in chronological order. The telling of stories enables people to bring order to difficult events, so they can better understand them and emotionally process them. Marginalised groups can define significant issues for them and their community (Plummer, 2001). The carer who was a gay man in particular was able to contextualise the impact of homophobia on the cared for and himself. Gibbs (2007: 57) suggests that stories have "dramatic and rhetorical force", as they are authoritative and their delivery conveys more meaning than the actual language. An example of this was when one carer's tone of voice suddenly changed and she sounded very angry about her mother's expectation that she should care for her.

Simons (2009) stresses the importance of the researcher needing to recognise themselves as the instrument of data collection, observations, interactions and the interplay of one's values and perceptions within the research process. As the researcher I was not disembodied but came with my personality, values, beliefs and expectations. One carer spoke at great length of her sadness about her mother's abandonment of her as a teenager and now her mother had dementia her mother would not be able to explain why she had behaved like this. I remember thinking that even without the dementia that her mother probably would not have been able to provide that explanation, and how sad that this daughter was so emotionally occupied by such an intractable difficulty. "It is when our emotions and feelings are aroused that we know our subjectivity is engaged" (Simons, 2009: 82), therefore my awareness of this was important so that I monitored my own emotional state, and its influence on the interaction. This was the carer's time to tell me her or his story from her or his own perspective without me offering advice, guidance or reassurance.

It is the carers' memories that organise the story into events, conversations and provide a time sequence. They understand their lives through the meanings that they give to events, for "human identity is narrational, lives being composed of the narratives by which time is experienced" (Erben, 1998: 11). Biographical research requires an understanding of the facts, the use of imagination and an analysis of the person's story by the researcher. Indeed Erben (1998) stresses that to be able to interpret and develop the ideas from the research into a coherent narrative imagination is required. This involves engaging with and trying to understand the experience of the carer, and starts with attentive listening through recognising the emotions being expressed and assessing if any themes are emerging. It also involves reflecting back what has been understood about the emotional impact of the interviewee's experiences, as well as checking that what is being told has been correctly understood.

It is Rogers's (1980) view that empathy is the most important factor in a relationship to support change and learning. This includes research and teaching as well as therapeutic interventions. He defines empathy as:

> to perceive the internal frames of reference of another with accuracy and with the emotional components and meanings which pertain thereto as if one were the person, but without ever losing the "as if" condition. Thus it means to sense the hurt or the pleasure of another as he (sic) senses it and to perceive the causes thereof as he (sic) perceives them, but without ever losing the recognition that it is as if I were hurt or pleased and so forth (Rogers, 1959 quoted in Rogers, 1980: 210-211).

To engage effectively with the carers needed my full attention and sensitivity so that I could, as Egan (2010:183) describes "tune in carefully, both physically and psychologically", while avoiding being over identified with the carer's emotional state, using my imagination but retaining an "as if" attitude (Rogers, 1959: 21; Erben, 1998). It also required me to be aware of my judgements and biases, as "bias comes not from having ethical and political positions – this is inevitable – but from not acknowledging them" (Griffiths, 1998: 133). I return to the concepts of bias and reflexivity later in the chapter.

Researcher as Guide

Atkinson (1998: 32) describes "the researcher as a guide" leading the participant through the interview by knowing what to ask, how to ask, the use of supplementary questions and recognising when there should be encouragement to give more information or to move on, as well as offering reassurance. Prior to our meeting most of the carers had made notes about what they wished to say on the interview schedule. One carer for instance provided photographs of his friend, and copies of documents relating to his contact with a local authority and the National Health Service, as he thought these would help me to understand his experience. This carer was guiding me; other carers had particular concerns that they wished to convey, or examples of how they had been effectively supported.

Rogers (1980) identifies the following elements that comprise effective communication skills: attentive listening, non-judgemental attitude, unconditional positive regard towards the person being interviewed, empathic understanding, genuineness and trust. The latter is achieved by treating information that is given by the participant as confidential. These approaches in attitude and behaviour are supported by the use of open questions that enable people to give expansive responses without being judged or contradicted by the researcher. I was persuaded by Atkinson (1988: 41) of the need for a "thematic framework" to questions that ensures that one theme is covered at a time, which focuses on thoughts, feelings and understandings, as the most effective approach. I was further guided in my approach by Atkinson's (1998: 34) attentive listening, which requires concentration but which raises the self-esteem of the participant in so far as "it gives people being listened to the feeling that they really matter, that what they have to say is important". Listening enables the researcher to build a "bridge of trust" between the researcher and participant, and inevitably "emotions emerge" (p.35). Most of the carers became emotional at some point in the interview, and for some they expressed their feelings of being upset, as if taken by surprise. Often during this time there was silence which can have different meanings such as the person feeling they have said enough on a topic, needing time to think, feelings of anger, self-protection and having shared information that is highly emotional and needing time to process it (Lishman, 2009). My observation was that some carers were overwhelmed by their feelings, and were finding it difficult to articulate them. Sometimes they expressed feelings of distress or anger about how they had been treated in the past by the cared for person or other people, while for others there was an intense sense of loss about the death of the person. I waited for the carers to indicate that they were ready to carry on, so they were in control of the pace of the interview.

Research is frequently evaluated in terms of how representative it is - the extent to which it reflects, or can be related to, the general population. In biographical research however, "insights, understandings, appreciation, intimate familiarity are the goals and not 'facts', explanations or generalizations" (Plummer, 2001: 153). When life stories are written they provide opportunities for interpretations and theorising, and information about the inner experience of the person. Even though anecdotal evidence is often denied validity, as stated earlier particular experience may have general or universal application on the experience of others (Simons, 2009). Some of the accounts that the carers gave had marked similarities: for example social care staff asking the carer to speak to the person with dementia about their behaviour, when it had presented problems for the care staff, as if the cared for person were a misbehaving child. There was little, or no, understanding on the part of the staff of the absurdity of the request, nor any reflection on what may have triggered the behaviour in the first place.

Returning to the concept of bias Griffiths (1998) identifies how bias can operate at different levels in research. To begin with the research process and procedures may have bias if particular groups of people are excluded or stereotyped. Bias can occur due to the values of the researchers and their political perspectives, and finally research that has been commissioned may require evidence to be produced that meets the funders' needs rather than the participants of the research. The carers were self-selecting with three criteria being in place which were that half the carers should identify as lesbian or gay, that they had retained a relationship with the person with dementia throughout the illness, and at least three of the carers had been caring in the last five years. The carers that approached me offering to be interviewed were, or had been in professional occupations; five were women with just one man, and they were all white. I used a range of methods to advertise for participants which included leaflets, web-sites, professional and personal networks. I was clear that for ethical reasons I wanted carers to offer to be participants. I did not wish to pressurise people, as I felt this to be wrong, as I suspected that the carers' stories would provoke strong emotional memories for them, which proved to be the case. Griffiths (1998: 129-130) explains: "Opinions give a clue to values ... Opinions set the research off and motivate it" which seem apposite comments on my own rationale for how I engaged with the participants, but in addition to this I visualised the interviews as being a source of great sorrow. I was uncertain if I could bear to hear these stories. It was the process of reflecting back on my "subjective selves" (Simons, 2009: 93) and using images to represent how I felt at the time that I have become aware of my apprehension, consequently I had to know that the carers really wanted to meet with me. The research was not externally funded, and therefore the requirements of commissioners were not an ethical issue that I had to confront and manage.

Oakley (1981) argues that effective interviews are achieved when the relationship between the researcher and the participant is non-hierarchical, and the researcher is prepared to provide some information about themselves, especially when people are being asked to disclose personal details. Oakley is highly critical of traditional social research interviews where the participant is passive, and is seen as a source of data. She maintains that the key role of the interviewer is to develop rapport and ask questions. Bias in the interview process is inevitable, and this needs to be recognised by the researcher and taken into account in the analysis of research findings:

> the mythology of 'hygienic' research with its accompanying mystification of the researcher and the researched as objective instruments of data production be replaced by the recognition that personal involvement is more than dangerous bias – it is a condition under which people come to know each other and admit others into their lives (Oakley, 1981: 58).

Malseed (2004) comments that Oakley's critique is unfair to social researchers, as a range of interview approaches can be used depending on the nature and purpose of the interview. Oakley (2004) commented in response to Malseed that often formal interviewing techniques are seen as the norm for traditional research subjects, whereas informal interview approaches are seen as deviations. One example of Oakley's research involved interviews with women about the transition to motherhood. To gather in depth information she needed to develop a personal relationship with the women to obtain their views about maternity and ante-natal services. Service improvements would not have come about without these insights. Further a lack of "bias in research could only be possible if researcher and informant were mechanical robots a researcher without a face to give off feelings" (Plummer, 2001: 156). On the other hand, Letherby (2004: 180) argues that: "a mutually exclusive divide between 'qualitative' and 'quantitative' is epistemologically debilitating as it results in a knowledge cul-de-sac." I have used statistical information pertaining to the incident of dementia, numbers of carers and their financial value to the UK economy, as this gives a context to the carers' stories, highlighting why the research is significant and relevant. Letherby (2004: 179) stresses: "it's not what you do but the way that you do it' that matters." This will be discussed in more detail in terms of ethical research practice.

Biographical research interviews such as those I engaged in are similar to getting to know someone socially where there will be a specific focus on exploring particular aspects of the person's life (Gearing and Dant, 1990). "Experience is the meaning maker in our lives" (Atkinson, 1998: 45), thus enabling people to talk about their experiences in an open and accepting manner gives them an opportunity to make sense of what has occurred, develops the person's self-awareness and enables them to articulate their learning from the experience. The biographical research method that I adopted "rests on a view of individuals as creators of meanings which form the basis of their everyday lives. Individuals act according to meanings through which they make sense of social existence" (Roberts, 2002: 6). I found this to be true for myself as the researcher, as the process gave me self-knowledge, as well as an understanding of carers' lives, and curiously the interviews were not as emotionally enervating as I had imagined.

Ethics as a Process

The subsequent recording and interpretation of the research findings need to be undertaken ethically. Clarke (1998), in her research account of the working lives of lesbian women teachers of physical education makes a powerful case, arguing that "how these stories are told is crucial if these seemingly private issues are to become public issues. Since how we write creates a particular and partial view of reality" (p.68).

How the carers' stories are presented is important as this will impact on their influence with a wider audience. To minimise the complexities of caring for someone with dementia presents the role of carers as unsubstantial, while focusing on the negative aspects of caring emphasises caring as a relentless burden. I wanted to be able to learn the different ways in which carers experience caring, and be able to identify health and social care practice that was positive, as well as unhelpful approaches.

The research framework integrated ethical principles into the design and delivery plan for the research. This drew upon the British Sociological Association's (2004) procedures for researchers, which includes ensuring that the interests of the interviewee are paramount and that informed consent is obtained. The concept of not harming participants through the research process is emphasised by the British Sociological Association:

> In many of its forms, social research intrudes into the lives of those studied. While some participants in sociological research may find the experience a positive and welcome one, for others the experience may be disturbing. Even if not harmed, those studied may feel wronged by aspects of the research process. This can be particularly so if they perceive intrusions into their private and personal worlds, or where research gives rise to false hopes, uncalled for self-knowledge, or unnecessary anxiety (British Sociological Association, 2004: 4).

Ethical practice is how we behave throughout every aspect of the research (Letherby, 2004). Although the research was approved through a university ethics committee such committees rarely check what has actually taken place during the course of the research and cannot 'govern ethical behaviour through forms and procedures' (Simons, 2009: 120). The principle of doing no harm could be expressed more positively by doing research *with* people rather than *to* them (Simons, 2009). Moreover the aim of the research should be "to minimize the harm or cost and maximise the benefit" (Gibbs, 2007: 101). This concurs with Griffiths' (1998: 129) research principle of "better knowledge" that improves the quality of people's lives and assists in the achievement of social justice. In spite of the time commitment for the carers, as well as the emotional impact of telling their stories, they were keen to participate, as they thought the telling of their stories could help other people. I regarded ethical practice in the research process as continuous and in need of ongoing evaluation as the research proceeded. The range of ethical issues that I was required to address as the researcher is presented in figure 3.1.

It was important that I made clear the aims and objectives of the research to the carers. Walmsley (1993: 47) states:

> In all research situations how we explain our research, and how the people being researched explain it to themselves is a subject worthy of attention, more attention than is usually given to it. It is a crucial determinant of what we discover.

Ethically the carers needed to understand the purpose of the research, and its limitations in terms of impact. The research was for academic purposes rather than having been commissioned by the Department of Health, so it was not likely to lead to policy or national practice changes within the health or social care professions.

Figure 3-1: Conceptual Ethical Framework

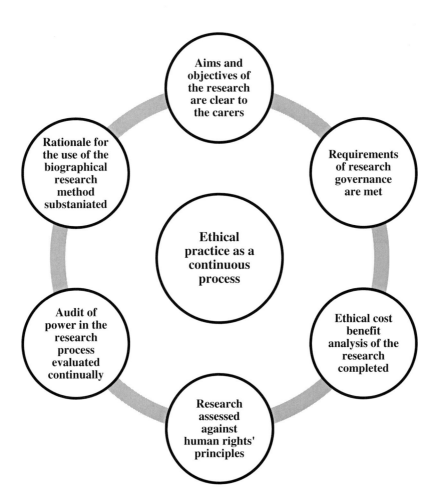

The carers gave informed consent in writing and, as stated I advised them that they could cease to be involved at any stage of the research without the need for explanation. Biographical interviews are likely to produce sensitive information from people who may feel vulnerable about aspects of their lives. There are issues of power between the researcher and participant, but I was mindful that the researcher always retains the real power as they have the data (Letherby, 2004). Because of this the transcript was sent to them for checking. The carers' privacy was respected and anonymity protected in the research through the substitution of their real names and geographical location with pseudonyms. Nevertheless it is important to recognise that the biographical approach provides personal and individualised information, so that carers could recognise themselves within the research. It is not possible to provide the same kind of anonymity that occurs in large scale quantitative research (Gibbs, 2007). A distinction needs to be drawn between confidentiality around personal and sensitive information that the researcher can be careful to protect and not discuss or use, and anonymity where names and places are changed, but inevitably the carer will recognise themselves and possibly other people will too (Simons, 2009). The carers were advised what would happen in the course of the research, how the data would be stored and managed. In spite of this, as the researcher I could not foresee how they might feel when reading the transcripts of the interview, even though I did anticipate that this may provoke concerns. In the event, only one carer requested something be changed.

An ethical dilemma highlighted by Etherington (2004) is when one person's story is bound up with another person. This was an issue for me, irrespective of whether the person with dementia was alive, or had died. Although most of the carers were compassionate and kindly in their descriptions of the person with dementia, one carer expressed extreme frustrations with the person, while another at times spoke with a disparaging tone. I recognised in part their comments reflected their disappointments about the person with dementia, either having never met their emotional needs, or no longer being able to do so. It still made me feel uncomfortable, as if I was colluding with the objectification and exclusion of the person with dementia as there was no one to speak up for them (Kitwood,1997).

In the following section I describe an ethical costs benefits analysis of the carers' engagement in the research.

Ethical Cost Benefit Analysis of the Research

Ethical considerations should be evaluated at every stage of the research (Liamputtong, 2007). The medical sciences have recognised that harm can occur through testing for example particular drugs or interventions, but more recently, as earlier discussed, it has been acknowledged that social science research can cause harm too (British Sociological Association,

2004). This has to be weighed up against not seeking the views of marginalised groups, and thereby denying them opportunities to be heard, which impacts on their capacity to achieve social justice (Griffiths, 1998).

It was possible to undertake a cost benefit analysis of the possible risks and benefits of the research to the carers. In this assessment, costs are defined as those things that have the potential to do harm, and benefits are activities that promote well-being. Liamputtong (2007) suggests that any research implications should be considered in terms of the personal, interpersonal, community and political impact of the research on the participant. These criteria have been used to evaluate the research and are represented visually in figures 3.2-3.5.

Figure 3-2: Cost Benefit Analysis of the Research

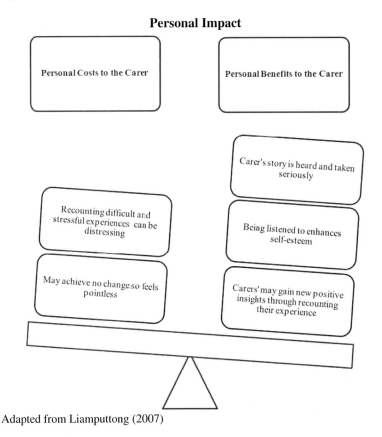

Personal Impact

| Personal Costs to the Carer | Personal Benefits to the Carer |

Carer's story is heard and taken seriously

Recounting difficult and stressful experiences can be distressing

Being listened to enhances self-esteem

May achieve no change so feels pointless

Carers' may gain new positive insights through recounting their experience

Adapted from Liamputtong (2007)

Figure 3-3: Cost Benefit Analysis of the Research

Interpersonal Impact

Interpersonal Costs to the
Carer

Interpersonal Benefits to the
Carer

Carer may reflect on how their
actions enhanced the well-being of
the cared for

Carers able to identify what was
helpful to them as a carer from
people and agencies, so they can
use this in other situations

May result in the articulation of
anger towards the cared for, family,
friends and agencies that is not
helpful to the carer

Carers' knowledge and
undestanding about dementia,
health and social care resources is
enhanced so they are better
informed

Adapted from Liamputtong (2007)

Figure 3-4: Cost Benefit Analysis of the Research

Community Impact

Community Costs to the Carer	Community Benefits to the Carer

Carers can talk about what supports them and think about engaging in community groups for carers

Lesbian women and gay male carers are 'outing' themselves through participation in the research and may be uneasy

Carers feel less isolated as they are aware that they are not alone in their community

Dementia is a stigmatised condition and carers may feel concerned about discussing a condition that affects a relative/friend

Through participation in the research carers are advised about community resources

Adapted from Liamputtong (2007)

Figure 3-5: Cost Benefit Analysis of the Research

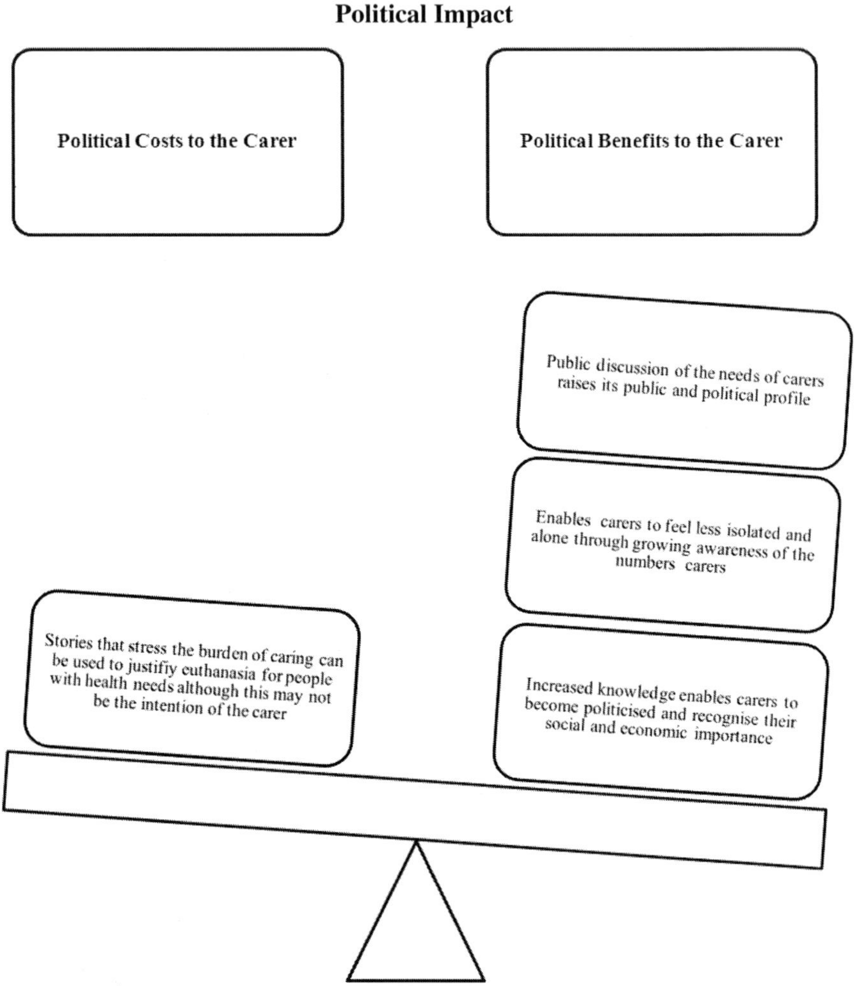

Political Impact

Political Costs to the Carer

Political Benefits to the Carer

Public discussion of the needs of carers raises its public and political profile

Enables carers to feel less isolated and alone through growing awareness of the numbers carers

Stories that stress the burden of caring can be used to justifiy euthanasia for people with health needs although this may not be the intention of the carer

Increased knowledge enables carers to become politicised and recognise their social and economic importance

Adapted from Liamputtong (2007)

The cost benefit analysis illustrates that there were positive reasons for the carers to be consulted about their experience that outweighed the negative impact for either them, the person for whom they cared, or on a wider social and political level. The impact of not engaging with particular groups, such as carers or people with dementia, reduces their capacity to articulate their concerns, and have their needs given social recognition and political priority, as their experience remains hidden and marginalised (Griffiths, 1998). A concern with human rights is "at the root of all emancipatory and anti-discriminatory research" (Witkin, 2000: 205). Three approaches to achieve this are: human rights as the goals of research, as evaluative criteria and as a guide to conducting research. The concept of human rights is the value placed on equality between people irrespective of health needs, sexuality, gender, ethnic and cultural origin, social class and marital status, consequentially Witkin (p.208) argues that: "Social research is a value-based culturally situated process whose knowledge claims are inherently political ... researchers both reflect and shape the social landscape." Research should provide "transformative criticism" that challenges assumptions and "generative theory" by offering alternative ideas and perspectives (Witkin, 2000: 211). These concepts were accepted as goals for my research and underpinned the messages for practice to health and social care services towards carers of people with dementia.

Self-Audit of Research Practice

There are differences in power and inequalities between people with dementia, carers, health and social care professionals. This revolves around hierarchies of knowledge and access to resources that can be heightened by differences in class, gender, age, sexuality, disability, culture and ethnic origin (Thompson, 2001). Braye and Preston-Shoot (1995) have developed principles to assess social care organisations against criteria of anti-oppressive practice so as to empower people that use services, and carers. Empowerment in this case is seen as a process that treats people with dignity and respect rather than objects to be controlled, manipulated or exploited. It comprises human rights, social justice and equality, which are the values that underpin social care practice (General Social Care Council, 2010). The following self- audit process (figure 3.6) has been adapted to assess my behaviour towards the carers at each stage of the research process. It also drew on the ethical requirements of the British Sociological Association (2004).

Figure 3-6: Self-Audit of Research Practice

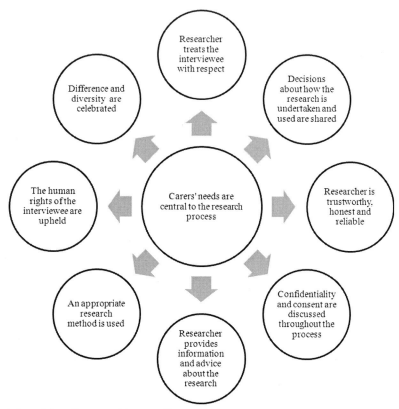

Adapted from Braye and Preston-Shoot (1995)

Throughout the research process I audited my ethical practice against the principles set out in figure 3.6, as ultimately the interview is based on collaboration between the interviewee and the researcher (Roberts, 2002). I sought to build and sustain a positive relationship with carers based on trust, and recognised the concept of "complex integrity" that requires the researcher to do more than simply follow ethical procedures (Simons, 2009: 110). This acknowledges the diversity of human experience, and that ethical practice should be our way of being not simply something we affect for the purposes of the research. Etherington (2004: 227) says "if we stumble carelessly into intimate personal research relationships we take the risk of leaving participants worse off by our encounters with them".

Participants may disclose information that they did not intend to, or have new insights that cause discomfort. The carers were advised that they could withdraw from the research process at any stage and all documentation would be destroyed. Furthermore, I gave the carers information about support services and resources pertaining to dementia and carers that they could access, if the interview had in anyway caused them distress. Ethical practice in the research process is intertwined with reflexivity, which enables an understanding to develop of how interactions with other people impact on us, and how we affect others (Schön, 1983). It is an "inner sense of knowing who we are and how we define what is important to us – those values, emotions and ways of thinking and being that affect how we live and act" (Simons, 2009: 82).

To support me in the process of making sense of the carers's stories I adapted Plummer's (2001: 251) evaluative questions, which assisted me to assess the similarities and differences between their stories. I used these questions, as reflection points when analysing the data.

- What moral dilemmas are happening here?

- Does the story have new insights?

- Who is telling the story?

- Who does it belong to?

- Who has been written out?

- Who are the other people in the life story?

- Does the story have depth and a broad context?

- Is the carer reflective?

- What truth claims are being made?

- Is the story located in time and place?

These evaluative questions were a valuable additional process to interrogate the findings that enabled me to assess my own interpretations, and reflect on my responses to the carers' stories. Gibbs (2007: 67) describes stories as being structured with a beginning, middle and end. In the course of the story they can "ascend" or "descend" depending on whether events are positive or problematic. Frank (1995) identifies three common stories relating to ill health: the restitution narrative where the person is ill but recovers; the chaos narrative where the person is ill and nothing improves and the quest narrative where the illness is like a journey where the person suffers, learns to overcome their difficulties and is finally restored having gained strength and wisdom. Stories do of course ascend and descend as they follow the story teller's memoires of events. For most of the carers their stories had ascended in the end. Many aspects of their stories contained the elements of quest narratives in the way that the carer told the story, notwithstanding this for one carer (Elaine) my interpretation of how she saw her story fitted more with the chaos narrative. These stories are hard to hear, as there is no resolution to the bleakness of the experience. We will now consider in detail the carers' stories of their experiences of supporting a person with dementia.

CHAPTER FOUR

CARERS' STORIES

Introduction

This chapter will centre on the lived experience of six carers that I interviewed, but it will be supported by other research findings. I will begin by giving information about the six carers including their relationship to the person with dementia. Their experiences are positioned within the social policy context as "a life that is studied is the study of a life in time" (Erben, 1998: 13), therefore the timeframe of caring was cross-referenced to successive pieces of legislation and policies that have sought to support carers and enable them to access services and resources.

The Carers

Table 4.1 below provides personal information about the carers. At the time of interview their ages spanned three decades, although for four of the carers the person with dementia had died. Two of the carers identified as lesbian women and one as a gay man. Two were heterosexual while one carer did not wish to disclose her sexuality.

Table 4.2 sets out the relationship between the carer and person with dementia. The five women carers were all supporting their mothers, and Theresa was caring for her father too. Nick was caring for a friend. The table provides information about where the cared for person lived. The table also provides information about the length of time people were caring.

The analysis of the carers' narratives has been placed in their social, political, cultural and personal context as this provides the opportunity to reflect on how these contexts have been influential on carers in terms of their caring experiences, the choices and opportunities available to them, as well as their strategies for coping (Erben, 1997).

Figure 4.1 locates the period of time the carers were caring in relation to legislation that has been developed to support carers. Each successive piece of legislation has entitled carers, at least in theory, to increased support such as an assessment of their needs; access to social care services; assistance to stay in employment or training, and the maintenance of leisure and social interests.

Table 4.1: Personal Information about the Carers

Carer	Age	Gender	Ethnic Origin	Sexuality	Partner	Occupation
Ruth	61	woman	British	lesbian	yes	university lecturer (retired)
Susan	53	woman	British	heterosexual	yes	social worker
Angela	60	woman	All White Groups	prefer not to say	no	student/ writer
Nick	72	man	British	gay	yes	university lecturer (retired)
Theresa	54	woman	British	lesbian	yes	retail manager (retired) health therapist
Elaine	51	woman	Welsh	heterosexual	yes	university lecturer / counsellor

Table 4.2: Relationship to the Person with Dementia

Name of Carer	Relationship to person with dementia	Region where person with dementia lives/d	Environment	Length of time caring for the person with dementia
Ruth	daughter	north west England	urban	6 years
Susan	daughter	south east England	urban	6 years
Angela	daughter	south east England	urban	on going
Nick	friend	London	urban	10 years
Theresa	daughter	north of England	urban	13 years
Elaine	daughter	Wales	rural	on going

Figure 4-1: Period of Time Caring

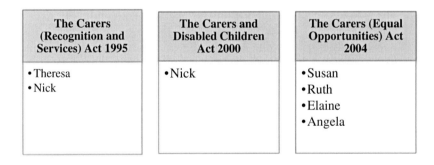

Significant changes have been made to legislation and social policy from the 1990s to 2000s with increased entitlements for carers through each additional piece of legislation. The Carers (Recognition and Services) Act 1995 gave new duties to local authorities to assess carers' needs and to take account of them in any services provided when the cared for needs were being assessed under the NHS and Community Care Act 1990. It did not entitle carers to have an assessment in their own right, so if the cared for did not want services from the local authority the carer could not be provided with support. This was addressed by the Carers and Disabled Children Act 2000, which enabled carers to have an assessment in their own right regardless of the views or wishes of the cared for. The Carers (Equal Opportunities) Act 2004 enables the needs of carers to be recognized in terms of work, training and education, in the same way as other citizens (Pierson & Thomas, 2010). Consequently carers who have recently been caring or are currently caring should have different experiences of health and social care services compared with carers, who were caring prior to legislation being implemented.

Profiling Individual Carers

Set down below is a brief profile of each individual carer, gathered through the questionnaire that they completed and the information that they gave to me. These profiles have been structured around family background, employment and the quality of the relationship with the cared for person.

Ruth

Ruth grew up with her mother, father and brother in the north west of England. Her relationship with her mother had always been difficult, as she was emotionally and physically abusive to Ruth and her brother as children. Following the death of her father Ruth became estranged from her mother. Her identification as a lesbian woman had created additional difficulties in her relationship with her mother.

Ruth was retired from an academic career and lived in the south east of England. She had acquired knowledge about health and social care services from her career and felt that she put that knowledge to good use in supporting her mother. She became a long distance carer to her mother following her mother's admission to hospital and diagnosis of dementia. Her brother, although living locally to his mother, was unable to maintain a relationship with her due to the impact of her emotional abuse. The co-ordination of care and management of practical tasks was managed between Ruth and her sister-in-law. When the interview took place Ruth's mother had died, so she was looking back at their relationship and the experience of being a carer.

Susan

Susan was brought up by her mother and father. She had an older sister and the whole family lived in the south east of England. Her relationship with her parents had been warm and very affectionate. When her father died she maintained a close relationship with her mother who lived locally, and found her a source of calm wisdom and support.

Susan was married with two adult sons. She was employed as a social worker working in a community team, primarily supporting older people. The onset of her mother's dementia meant that Susan lost a trusted confidant, as she noticed slight changes to how her mother responded to her. The poor quality of care that Susan's mother received, delivered by private sector domiciliary care agencies, precipitated Susan moving into her mother's home and caring for her. Susan experienced social work services from the perspective of a carer and found them wanting. At the time of the interview Susan's mother had died, so she like Ruth was looking back on her experience of caring.

Angela

Angela was an only child. In her completion of the questionnaire about herself she was reluctant to disclose too much information of a personal nature. She was a lone parent with two teenage children, one of whom had learning difficulties. Angela's mother had always been a very sociable woman, who made demands of her husband in terms of attention. Following his death her mother assumed that Angela would fulfil her father's role by supporting her emotionally.

When her mother was diagnosed with dementia Angela moved herself and the children into her mother's home. In many senses Angela felt as if she had no choice but to do this, as it was what her mother demanded. The relationship was clearly complex, and stressful for Angela, especially as the dementia progressed. She was a part-time mature student and wrote for a publication, and these activities including her interest in art offered some respite from caring for her mother. At the time of the interview Angela's mother had settled into a care home locally. Angela visited her on a regular basis, and identified her admission to care as the most helpful service to her as a carer.

Nick

Nick was brought up by his parents in Wales, and has a brother. He became carer to his friend of 40 years, Simon. Both men identified as gay, but they had never been partners. Nick was a retired academic working and living in London.

Nick provided support to Simon over the course of his illness, and was the only consistent carer that he had. Simon's family was neglectful, and found it difficult to accept his sexuality. Nick's friendship with Simon was of long duration, and he was able to provide person centred and creative approaches to support his friend, and enhance his well-being. The total rejection and exclusion of Nick by Simon's family clearly had a considerable emotional impact. Social Services failed to support Nick, which resulted in Nick successfully complaining against Social Services and being awarded compensation following the involvement of the Office of Local Administration (Ombudsman), which Nick gave to charity. Nick, like Ruth and Susan, used his professional skills to access resources and advocate for Simon. At the time of the interview Simon had died and Nick was reflecting back on his experiences.

Elaine

Elaine was brought up by parents in Wales with a younger sister. Her mother left the family when Elaine was thirteen years old, and Elaine took on the role of caring for her father and sister. Both parents appear to have found life problematic and Elaine felt a heavy weight of emotional and practical responsibility at a young age. This culminated in her having a 'breakdown' as a young woman and leaving Wales. She did return only to leave again, due to the demands that her mother made on her. By this time Elaine had married and had her own children. Elaine felt that her mother had abandoned her and her sister when she left the family having met another man. Elaine's professional background as a social worker and counsellor gave her a particular insight into her own emotional development, as well as a strong sense of what was ethically right to do in terms of her mother's plight. Although she lived in the south east of England Elaine phoned and visited her mother in Wales on a regular basis, and worked with her sister to provide as much support as possible. Elaine's mother had recently been admitted to a care home, as she had become isolated and lonely living a home.

Theresa

Theresa was an only child, who became a carer in her thirties. This was initially for her mother and then for her father. She had a successful career which necessitated her moving around Britain. Her father had worked for the same company, and much of the time she lived with her parents, who moved with her. Theresa had a deep emotional attachment to both parents, and realised that they would be unhappy if they were separated, so she chose to care for them both at home, as she recognised that the family did not have sufficient financial resources to purchase high quality care in a nursing home. Theresa took redundancy from the company, and provided care to both parents that included nursing tasks. Following her parents' death Theresa resolved to find a partner and settle down. When interviewed Theresa was able to discuss her experience of caring as well as the experiences of other lesbian, gay, bisexual and transgender people that she had supported through a national organisation for people with dementia and their carers.

The Experience of Caring

I started by seeking to understand how the carers had chosen to continue their involvement with the person, and accept their role as a carer. It appeared to me that this was a turning point or epiphany in so far, as a decision was made either consciously or otherwise to continue with the relationship, and an acceptance that the relationship would change. This enabled me to begin the process of understanding about the experience of caring. The first example of turning points relates to Elaine who had always felt she was her mother's carer, and comes from an earlier time in her life.

Elaine's memory of always being a carer to her mother was "transformative remembering" (Plummer, 2001: 237) as her increased self-awareness enhanced her understanding of her relationship with her mother, and the impact that it had on her emotionally. Elaine felt trapped by the emotional needs of her mother and there was a role reversal. She mothered her mother and felt responsible for her. A turning point occurred when Elaine left Wales to create some physical distance between herself and her mother. This was for Elaine a "major turning point", as defined by Denzin (1989:71) as it impacted on every area of her life. She realised that by leaving her mother she would no longer be drawn into her emotional and practical difficulties:

> I think probably when I was twenty five I eventually decided that something had to give, but during that time I had also got married and divorced and decided that I wanted to go away and do something ... I was getting back into the patterns, the old ways of being ... so I made the deliberate choice to move to England ... She's [her mother] had lots of crisis in her life ... I would go and visit and find that her and her new partner had split up, so she'd need a lift to her new accommodation, or

> she'd want to go back to my father ... There was also things like not taking
> responsibility for paying bills, or the practical day to day things you need
> to do in order to either run a home or just to sustain living.

There is some similarity between the strategies Elaine used to deal with a
problematic relationship, and those of Ruth.

Ruth left the north west of England, and moved to the south east as Elaine
had done, but unlike Elaine she ceased to have contact with her mother.
This was due to the verbal, emotional and sometimes physical abuse of
Ruth's mother. Ruth's mother was admitted compulsorily to a psychiatric
hospital, and she was contacted as the next of kin following her mother's
hospital admission. Her mother's house had become home to feral cats; the
toilet was blocked and there were several hundred bottles of sour milk
found in the house. The hospital admission and poor condition of the
house became "representational acts" (Denzin, 1989:71) as this was a
crisis, and it became a turning point when Ruth's mother asked for her
help to stay at home rather than be admitted to institutional care. Ruth
made the decision to re-establish a relationship with her mother, as she
realised that her mother was fearful of institutions, as she remembered the
cultural legacy of long stay hospitals for people with mental health needs
and learning disabilities (Means *et al.*, 2008).

There was another "major turning point" (Denzin, 1989: 71) for Ruth with
the sudden realisation about her relationship with her mother and her sense
of self:

> you see this once very powerful person is now a frail, little person, little
> old vulnerable person, for all their rage and anger that they're still able to
> show. Because the rage and the anger earlier in life were the things that
> terrified you of her, but you start to see them differently, and so it puts you
> in a completely different position, and I suppose you see yourself
> differently in that case yeah? So you realise that actually you are capable
> of a lot of compassion and forgiveness, and that actually feels quite good.

Interestingly Ruth speaks in the second person as if looking at herself and
her mother objectively from a distance. Ruth and Elaine both became long
distance carers separated by several hundreds of miles, although they both
were actively involved in working with other family members, social and
health services to support their mothers. Angela's relationship with her
mother was fraught following the death of her father as her mother
expected her to move into her home, although she had two adolescent
children. These three carers felt a family obligation to care, that Means *et*

al. (2008) suggest has been reinforced through government policy that strengthens a cultural norm.

Susan, Nick and Theresa had less complex relationships with the cared for person, as there were strong emotional ties of many years' duration. Susan described her mother as: "the lynchpin of the family. She was the most wonderful mother, a lovely mum, very unassuming, very gentle." She felt that she was returning to her mother the care that she had received all her life. Theresa was an only child whose parents had a very close relationship and would not have been able to live happily apart. The impact of dementia on her mother was that: "if anything she became sweeter in character. She was always a lovely lady, but somehow she became the essence of sweetness." For Susan a major turning point came when she moved into her mother's home to care for her, due to the inadequate care provided by a domiciliary care agency, similarly for Theresa, who gave up her career so she could care for her parents.

Nick experienced a series of "minor events" (Denzin, 1989:70) that became a turning point when he understood that his friend, Simon, would not receive any emotional or practical support from his family because of his sexual identity as a gay man. Nick stepped into the role of carer, and this was for many years reinforced by health and social care services, who involved him in care planning and acting as an advocate for Simon, until the family requested that this level of engagement cease.

Changes in Relationships

The historical context of the relationship and its continuation, as the dementia in the cared for progresses, are significant. The proximity to the cared for as well as familial relationships are often determining factors in terms of whom is seen as the main carer in an hierarchy of relationships used by health and social care services (Finch and Groves,1983; Letherby, 2002). This concept enabled Simon's family to request that Nick's involvement with Simon be reduced to simply visiting him on the hospital ward rather than supporting him more fully even though the family only visited Simon very infrequently. Nick believed this attitude developed due to the family perceiving Simon as "blemished" (Goffman, 1963: 20) as he was a gay man. The family also had concerns that they should be sole recipients of his inheritance.

Elaine's younger sister received more communication about her mother than she did, as she lived near her mother. As Ruth's sister-in-law was local to her mother she was called upon in the event of difficulties. The distance from the person with dementia was a factor in how health and social care services worked with the carer. Bytheway *et al.* (1998) found that time as well as proximity was significant in terms of who cares. Ruth had a brother and sister-in-law that lived locally, as did Elaine, while Susan's husband and sister supported her. Theresa, Angela and Nick were lone carers.

The child carers' relationship with their parent/s changed as their emotional and physical dependency increased as the dementia progressed. Angela spoke of her frustration with her mother who followed her around the house. She was also irritated by her constant repetition. She described her mother as always being "really possessive" with a tendency towards jealousy which had resulted in her father calling her "the green eyed monster". This behaviour intensified over time, although she felt able to manage the behaviour of her son who had special needs:

> I've endless patience with my son, and it always amazed me that I couldn't have the same sort of patience with my mother but I didn't ... I think one expects one's parents to always be better, superior, more able, more composed than one is oneself.

This change in the dynamics of the relationship finds resonance in Susan's comments. She felt guilty that she had failed to realise that her mother was developing dementia, but noticed that the quality of their relationship was different:

> Inside you know, not something that you can speak about, but you just notice that there is a reason that you are withdrawing from someone, it's that they're not able to give you something that they used to before.

Susan noticed that her sister was "struggling" caring for her mother and she increased her involvement when she perceived that things were problematic and finally moved in with her mother to provide care.

Elaine spoke of her immense sadness about her mother following the diagnosis of dementia of "losing her all over again" when there may have been a chance for a different and closer relationship. Elaine spoke with emotion of finding:

some sort of resolution and recognising that I couldn't, because I couldn't have what I wanted I had to love and respect and cherish the bits of her that I loved. She is my mother, I will always love her ... but she could never be what I wanted her to be ever.

Elaine's regret about her relationship with her mother was a consistent theme:

I couldn't ever make her have a relationship with me in the way I wanted you know you can't make somebody else do that can you? You can only go with what they are giving or offering, and she didn't have much to offer really you know.

In the past Elaine's mother had cancelled social arrangements with her daughters if a better social outing was on offer, but now their mother was socially dependent on them. Therefore there were changes in the power and the control in the relationship.

Nick spoke with great compassion about the changes wrought on his friend Simon by the illness, especially the poor quality care he experienced in dilapidated NHS in-patient provision. He recalled that in one psychiatric hospital, which is now closed, Simon's clothes had to be destroyed, as he became infected with lice on three occasions. Nick was witness to his friend's increased cognitive and physical decline in care environments that were environmentally depressing, but he continued to visit. "I would come back sometimes and I would be terribly despondent, I might weep, you know what on earth am I going to do about this?"

Simon's psychiatrist was supportive and hopeful. He told Nick that what was needed was "social medicine" and that a great deal could be done to enhance Simon's life. Nick fulfilled this by visiting Simon in different care settings, and took him out to social places such as a familiar gay pub where they played a simple game of dominos. Nick stated that when he asked Simon if he was happy, he would reply: "happy when I am with you." Their friendship was of long duration and provided a bed rock for Nick's continued involvement. He described Simon as someone who:

had a lot of care for the underdog yes, he'd always been a kind person and somebody who would, I mean if somebody was being attacked in the street he would go in and have a go, or if you were driving past it would be, 'stop the car we have to go and help those people!' Now that's something that not everyone else might do, so I think it became more pathetic, it was still there, but it became even more poignant and pathetic, when he was in this desperate state in a way.

Simon's sexuality was usually ignored, and did not feature in the care and support that he received apart from the day centre he attended, who took an interest in his life story, and established a support group for lesbian women and gay male carers. The general lack of interest in Simon's sexuality confirms the view that "old equals asexual" (Thompson, 2001: 90) and encapsulates the ageist view that to be older is to be less than human, whereas sexuality shapes identity, self-image and social relations. At a structural level there are implications for lesbian women and gay men who in the past have experienced discrimination and oppression through state institutions (Ward *et al.,* 2005). Simon's family viewed his sexual identity as stigmatised, and his life story as a gay man was known by Nick alone. The importance of a shared history has multiple benefits for the person with dementia, as it preserves their sense of identity, provides reassurance and comfort.

> As dementia progresses, it becomes more difficult to hold on to the stories of one's life and to be able to tell others of the defining moments that shaped our identity. One of the jobs of caring for someone with dementia is to learn these key stories and hold this narrative for them. This can be used to improve self-esteem and to maintain an identity in the face of increasing confusion (Brooker, 2007: 58).

This has resonance for all people with dementia, but there are particular implications for a lesbian woman or gay man, as their cultural history may be ignored, marginalised or devalued. Nick sought to provide Simon with a continued sense of himself and happy memories as a gay man by putting photographs up in his room on the ward of their outings, work colleagues and familiar places. On one of the rare occasions that Simon's family visited they took these photographs down and replaced them with photographs of Simon with a girl he had last seen forty-five years ago and his sister, and family weddings, which had no meaning for Simon. Nick stated: "There it was Simon is *not* a gay man." Nick interpreted the action as unkind and a denial of who Simon was, as it produced confusion and was removing from Simon his life story, and images which he could relate to that gave him pleasure.

Theresa was 36 years old when she became a carer to her mother aged 61 years and her father who was 65 years old. She had tried to tell her mother about her sexuality when she was in her twenties, but her mother did not want to discuss it. It then became too late due to her mother's dementia, and her life "went into a complete hold as a carer." She explained that she had "a rather closeted and somewhat limited life when it came to sexuality." Theresa adopted a pragmatic and highly organised approach to the change in her relationship with her parents. She gave up a career and worked hard to meet her parents' needs by living with them, until they died. She ensured that their usual pattern of family life continued for as long as possible through outings and holidays until this was no longer possible. Theresa took up Tai Chi taking her parents with her. Theresa's transition into being a carer displays no sense of regret for time lost. Her engagement and commitment to both her parents were highly apparent even though her father who outlived her mother had multiple needs and could be "un-cooperative."

Being Remembered

One result of dementia that can be especially difficult for carers is the anxiety that the person will forget who they are. This was expressed by Ruth:

> I suppose one has a particular, well horror is the wrong word I suppose, but concerns that somehow the person is suddenly not going to know you or something like this. But that didn't happen to her, she always knew who I was.

Clearly it had been important and significant to Ruth that her name or presence was never forgotten. Nick described Simon's delight at seeing him. Simon would spring up from his seat, giving him a hug and greet him by name enthusiastically. Susan, Angela and Theresa stated that their mothers remembered them. Elaine phoned her mother each day, and she always recognised her voice, but she thought that her mother was having difficulty in remembering her in person, as she had adopted an approach that she had seen her use with other people:

> she ... employed that way she speaks when she meets people on the street, you know, 'oh hello, and how are you, I haven't seen you for a long time.' Which is what she says to people when she kind of knows she recognises them but hasn't seen them for a long time, and is not sure who they are. That hurts, that definitely hurts.

This is a common factor for carers and may impact on how close they feel to the person with dementia, and equate this with a loss of love. Bryden (2005:109), who has dementia, suggests:

> I know faces and know I connect with them somehow, but not why I know them and what I know about them. It is a world in which I know that I

know you, but not why I know you. I need time and clues, not questions.
Try to chat about our shared experiences, so that I can find out why I know
you.

This was an approach that Elaine was beginning to use with her mother.
She felt that her mother was remembering her sister and her children more
than her own. This made Elaine feel envious especially as her mother was
telling her sister things about her background that had never been
discussed before. There had been some tension between Elaine and her
sister and ongoing discussions about who takes responsibility for what.
Elaine was keen to play her part, and supported her mother to create a life
story book with the use of photographs to capture her memories of the
past. She recalled that her mother felt she had lost her family due to her
parents' death, as if Elaine and her sister and their children were not
family. Morris and Morris (2010: 44) write of the "felt experience of
carers" of distress and loneliness when some memoires can no longer be
shared. The identity of the carer is bound together with the cared for
person. Elaine's ambivalence about whether her mother had felt
unconditional love for her was being raised again by her suspicion that her
mother was starting to forget her, and would soon no longer recognise
Elaine's children.

Ruth's response to the change in her relationship with her mother was to
work out areas of responsibility with her sister-in-law and organise
practical aspects with considerable effectiveness ensuring that her mother
received technological aids and adaptations, and appropriate domiciliary
care services that could meet her needs. There was conflict as her brother
and sister-in-law wanted her mother to be placed in a care home, primarily
as there were a range of practical problems; for example, the Fire Brigade
was called as foil had been placed on food in the microwave and heated
for some time causing smoke in the kitchen. Also, she was reluctant to
take any medication, receive personal care or use services such as day
care. Ruth reflected on her brother and sister-in-law's anxiety:

> I used to feel quite guilty as I was the one who insisted she stay at home,
> it's causing their stress, and it's causing me stress, but you know there's
> our mum who just wants to stay at home with her cat, you know a difficult
> balance.

Susan also had difficulties with her relatives, who thought that her mother
should be in a care home. Her mother stayed with her aunt for a short
holiday, which Susan had advised against as she anticipated that this

would confuse her further, however she was overruled by her aunt. The stay was highly problematic:

> My cousin rang and said I was ill treating mum, how dare I not have her in a home ... mum got so distressed that she started to crawl, which was behaviour I had never seen before, around my aunt's house. So I went and picked mum up and my aunt said, 'we must be ill treating her to be going around on the floor on all fours.'... all that part of the family, mum's sisters and my cousins who have been close to my mum, didn't come to the funeral even and have not spoken to us since.

Susan interpreted their behaviour as an indication of their ignorance about dementia.

Nick was keen that Simon should be remembered by his family, so that his sense of identity could be strengthened, but his request to the family to visit Simon and send him a card at Christmas and so on went unheeded. He placed an advertisement in Simon's home town's local paper asking, if anyone knew him as a child. He received a number of letters from local people, and he found an Irish society in London that they both could attend. This provided pleasurable social events and enabled Nick to develop a greater understanding of Simon's childhood, and build up "little islands of memories" that he could talk to Simon about. Nick felt that the family in Ireland may have become embarrassed that Simon was living in a care home and felt some unease about his sexuality. The result was that the family asked Social Services and the NHS to ensure that Nick was not to take Simon out, or have any involvement in his care. Nick explained "Simon's life without these things is so much poorer, he loves going out, this is his life."

Although Nick was Simon's main carer the family's views were paramount, as he was caring prior to the implementation of the Mental Capacity Act 2005, which would have provided an opportunity to assess the appropriateness of the family's views and involvement. It is clear why Simon chose to hold "dual identities" (Clarke, 1996: 196) rather than being an openly gay man at work and with his family due to societal and hostile family attitudes (Dick, 2009). Theresa and Angela as only children were sole carers. They assumed responsibility for their parents and although this was stressful and at times isolating they did not need to negotiate with siblings or with other family members.

Social and Emotional Isolation

The carers were all aware of the increased social isolation of the cared for as the dementia progressed. Although Elaine's mother had always been very sociable, a "bright and intelligent" woman who loved music and dancing, since the onset of dementia her closest friend was unable to cope with her repetitive speech, and the fact that she would get on the wrong bus when they planned to meet. In the case of Ruth's mother she had struggled with relationships throughout her life. There had been a friend who visited down the road but her mother would be "bad mouthing her as soon as she had gone ... she didn't really appreciate people."

Angela's mother had a wide circle of friends, but now she only saw them once or twice a year. She had become deaf and had difficulty wearing her hearing aids so this "closed her off from communication." The carers recognised the increased dependency on them as one of the most significant social relationships that the person with dementia had, so carers too felt socially isolated due to supporting the person with dementia. Theresa spoke of an aunt and cousins who would on occasions come over and sit with her parents so she could go out:

> They didn't want to do any hands on caring; they didn't want any of that. They were always very keen to get away at the end of it, which I can understand fully. And I appreciated the bits they did, but I did get very tired of being told how good I was ... I don't want to be an angel, I felt so angry all the time I could punch somebody, but who have I got to actually do that with and to, how do I release it?

This view was echoed by Susan: "I think one of the other things that really started to annoy me, was that everybody started to pity me." She went on to speak of her own social isolation:

> Friends dropped off, we used to be invited out for meals, and I used to go out for meals with people. We couldn't invite people home, because there wasn't enough space, and also I felt that it would be worrying for mum. So we didn't manage to do that, and I realised the knock on effect of that, mainly after mum died, was that we'd lost friends, we retained good friends but I also had not realised the knock on effect for my children. Both were going through some difficult times and they only had scant time from me, and when I was ready to start being mum again they had moved on and it's taken a time for me to establish my relationship with them.

Susan experienced a sense of guilt towards her own children, which is a theme that re-emerges, and finds a resonance with Elaine's expressed guilt for not bringing her mother into her own home to be cared for. I felt that their expectations of themselves were harsh given that they both had or were providing substantial practical and emotional care. It was as if they were measuring themselves against a gendered stereotype of what is both a moral and biologically driven understanding of what it means to be a woman. This reminded me of Hanmer and Statham's (1988: 62) view – "caring for adults is taken to be as natural for women as caring for children. Because this view is often internalised, if the act of caring is unsuccessful, women blame themselves. The failure is personalised." Moreover Lafrance and Stoppard (2007) argue that the social and political position of women creates a narrative of the "good woman identity" (p.30), which I sensed both Susan and Elaine assessed themselves against.

Enduring Aspects of Relationships

The carers were able to identify examples of fulfilling activities and factors about their relationship with the cared for person. Humour was mentioned by several carers. Ruth said of her mother: "she had a good sense of humour she could laugh, although she was quite eccentric!" Elaine was able to engage with her mother in a humorous manner:

> we have a similar sense of humour so we would meet at that level, and maybe laugh over something that's silly ... because she has a great sense of humour I think that's partly where I get my sense of humour from.

Theresa spoke of maintaining a pattern of activities for her parents so they were physically and socially active:

> We went out virtually every day, because I'm a great believer, just as my parents before me in fresh air, and it transpired you know, being out in the sunshine and fresh air it makes for a better sleeping pattern at night. So they weren't particularly fractious at night, in fact my mother didn't try and wander at night ... they went out to family parties, we went out every day. We would go and visit places that wasn't an issue, this was part of normal life. My father was in a wheelchair, we did go on holiday with him in a wheelchair so that we could go to the seaside ... I was never ever going to try to limit their lives because of the health issues that they had.

Theresa consistently expressed the importance she attached to the maintenance of the quality of her parents' lives together, so as well as introducing new activities such as Tai Chi, she continued with a similar pattern of daily life for as long as possible. Nick spoke about his friendship with Simon:

> you imagine having a friend and you could call in any hour of the day or night and say, 'We are going to Greenwich' 'Yes! Let's go now!' We don't have friends like that for the most part, so anything you wanted to do, it was, 'Yes! Let's do it now where's my coat?' And although Simon might be surly and difficult with some people, he never was with me. And that was very, very positive, and also I thought that the quality of his thought and feeling at times with this massive limitations were just very fine, and he would see somebody ... who was having a difficult time, he'd go and just put his hand around them and just say 'what's the matter?' and he was just not capable of taking in what was the matter, but just to comfort them.

Nick and Simon especially enjoyed activities that took them out of the care environment in the same way that Theresa's parents benefited from the stimulation of being out of the house. These perspectives contrast with those of Angela, who had always experienced her mother as requiring a lot of attention a demand which had been met by her father while he was alive, but with the onset of dementia her mother became "increasingly anxious and increasingly repetitive." As time went on Angela found it more difficult to remove herself from her mother to read quietly. She felt considerable relief when her mother moved into a care home, whereas Susan was able to recount moments of intense joy with her mother:

> we got at a relationship a lot of the time where we had enormous fun, because I realised if we joined in her communication needs, we spent an awful lot of time laughing and doing daft things, what about? I haven't a clue! But we seemed to enjoy ourselves together.

A number of the carers used their knowledge of the cared for to build on areas of interest or pleasure. Ruth recognised that the common ground for anyone trying to develop a relationship with her mother was to talk about animals. For Elaine it was her mother's pleasure in music and horses. Nick ensured that Simon could watch musicals in the care home, as these had a calming effect and gave Simon great pleasure. Most of the carers were able to identify how their personal knowledge of the cared for enabled them to create, as Nick stated 'little islands of memory in this great sea of confusion' which maintained and supported positive aspects of the relationship between the carer and person with dementia.

In the accounts that the carers gave there were examples of how they were able to "tune in carefully, both physically and psychologically" (Egan, 2010: 183) so they could understand the perspective of the person with dementia. This enabled them to sense how the person was feeling and why they behaved in particular ways. Many of the carers showed empathy, which is paramount in building and sustaining relationships (Rogers, 1980). The relationship between the cared for person and the carer is fundamental to how the experience of caring is perceived (Burton, 2008). Angela found caring for her mother was stressful and for Ruth troublesome and worrying, whereas the other carers were able to identify the demands and difficulties but also the aspects of the relationship that remained rewarding. I will now consider the coping strategies that carers used that enabled them to continue to care.

CHAPTER FIVE

COPING APPROACHES

Introduction

In this chapter I will consider the approaches that the carers used to manage the needs of the person with dementia, and their own needs. This often required them to adjust their behaviour and be flexible, which I have linked to their belief systems and personal values. The chapter will reflect the experiences of the six carers that I interviewed, as well as other research. The definition of coping that I will use in the chapter is as follows:

> [coping is] a process of shifting behaviours, thoughts, and feelings that individuals use in interaction with their situations to avoid being harmed by life stressors (Abbott, cited by Canda, 2009: 87).

The approaches that are used by carers contained similarities and differences, and these will now be explored.

Approaches to Stress

The coping approaches used by carers of people with dementia are developed through values, beliefs, attitudes, understanding and experience which then impact on their behaviour. Folkman and Lazarus (1984, quoted by Norman *et al.,* 2004: 20) define coping as "the cognitive and behavioural efforts to manage specific external and/or internal demands appraised as taxing or exceeding the resources of the individual". This definition as the one above emphasises the demands on the individual to manage especially complex and stressful circumstances; as already identified there are particular complexities in caring for someone with dementia (Perren *et al.,* 2006). Carers in research by Perren *et al.* described the difficulties of adjusting and their feelings of loss as their partner's sense of identity changed, and the emotional distress of not being recognised by them. For many as the dementia became more advanced they lost friendships, independence and a sense of self worth. Additional difficulties were also evident by the decline of physical health with ageing, and the onset of depression caused by the diagnosis of dementia. One coping approach identified by people with dementia and their carers was acceptance, which included a philosophical approach to active engagement in civil rights campaigning. The support of family and friends, with specialist advice, information and assistance from health and social care services were also seen as essential. A further strategy of coping was a sense of humour (Williamson, 2008).

Carers may not identify themselves as carers, and indeed might resent this categorisation. Carers can feel guilt if the cared for person no longer lives with them this particularly impacts on women (Hanmer and Statham, 1988). Ungerson (1987) found that male carers tended to see their caring role as if it were a job. This enabled them to achieve some emotional distance from the strains of caring. This finds resonance in Marriott's (2003: 76) work on being a male carer to his wife, who lives with Huntington's disease:

> Carers who think of themselves as valued professionals are much less vulnerable than those who see themselves simply as relations or good neighbours.
>
> If you are professional, you're protected from some of those wounding self-doubts. There's a bit of distance between you and some of the hardest-to-bear aspects of caring. And when you itch to be doing another job, or living another life, then reflecting on the importance of the one you've been landed with may help your frame of mind.

It is a common sense notion that where the relationship between people prior to the dementia has been affectionate and mutually supportive, carers are motivated to sustain their relationship over time. Interestingly some carers, primarily daughters and sons, have stated that their relationship with their parent improved as a result of the dementia:

> I never imagined I would be grateful for any illness. But my mother, who never was a real mother, never baked cookies after school or told me she loved me, never played with me or thought I was pretty or bright. She was jealous of me and my dad, said mean and hateful things … she wanted a son, you see. I guess I was the competition. She never really took to me. Now she loves me, she really does! She stands at the door and throws her arms open and smiles and smiles and hugs me tighter than I could imagine. 'Here's my girl', she says (Lipinska, 2009: 56).

Menzies's (2009) account of caring for her mother with dementia, and the effect that this has on her and her siblings, demonstrates a similar transformation in her relationship. Her mother lacked emotional warmth towards her children. She was a domineering parent, but dementia enabled a very different type of relationship to develop:

> I'd discovered the lovely landscape of sitting side by side with Mum on her single residence bed, just holding hands. When a stroke and a broken hip took her down further, we became so attuned to each other it was though the umbilical cord that had connected us at the beginning of my life had grown back between us at the end of hers (p.9).

These examples provide an interesting insight into the interdependency between adult daughters and their mothers. The case histories of Stokes (2008) explicate problematic behaviour of people with dementia through the use of biography and an understanding of their personality. They demonstrate the range of responses that partners in particular have towards the person with dementia. These ultimately determine the nature and duration of support provided. Many carers feel that they have lost the person they once knew and loved, and that someone else is in their place. Kitwood (1997: 141) suggests this stops carers from being able to mourn and prevents the "growth of a new kind of relationship more empathic and intuitive than before". This requires carers to be able to accept the changes that the illness has bought while recognising and responding to the continued emotional needs of the person. Malthouse (2011) writes of her epiphany when she accepted the impact of dementia on her mother's speech which had become repetitive; instead of being irritable and trying to fight the consequences of the illness she accepted the changes in her mother's behaviour.

Askham *et al.* (2007) used participant observation and interviews with twenty carers. They analysed the data against Goffman's (1961) definitions of the characteristics of institutional care: routinisation of daily activities: surveillance of the person's behaviour and enforcement of self, that is, the carer maintaining a distance or expressing open hostility. All these behaviours were found, the most extreme being physically abusive, and all illustrate Kitwood's (1997: 45) "malignant social psychology". The researcher wrote in field notes:

> During a conversation about politics, the grandmother with dementia said,
>
> 'Tony Blair [the British Prime Minister] used to live in the flat below me.' There was first silence and then three responses: (i) Mrs Y (grandson's mother-in-law) looked at the speaker and said, ' Don't be stupid, of course he didn't'; (ii) R (granddaughter) quickly said in a soft voice, 'Oh, did

he?'; and (iii) B (son) said laughing, ' Don't be draft, he lived in Islington'
(Askham *et al.*, 2007: 16).

The granddaughter's empathy for her grandmother is contrasted starkly
with the disparagement and mockery of the other family members,
although there are examples of carers displaying compassion within the
research. To use Goffman's definitions of institutional relationships is a
particularly bleak frame of reference, as interactions and behaviours are
assessed against these negative constructs, without any counterbalance of
positive interactions. This could impact on the focus of the research.

The importance of specialist training in dementia care was highlighted in
research by Scott *et al.* (2011) involving analysis of questionnaires
responses from 112 nurses and care assistants supporting people with
dementia in care homes in Northern Ireland. They found that 69% had
been involved in an incident where they feared for their safety, 71%
witnessed an incident where they were anxious about the safety of a
colleague, 34% had felt unsafe and 18% terrified. In 17% of incidents the
person with dementia had used an object such as a walking stick, zimmer
frame, shoes, crockery and chairs. The triggers for aggression were getting
the person with dementia out of bed, preventing fights amongst residents
and stopping unsafe activities such as tampering with electrical equipment.
The triggers were known in half of the incidents, whereas a number of the
incidents the staff reported had happened unexpectedly. The researchers
concluded that some of the incidents had occurred because "sensitive
situations requiring diplomacy appear to have been handled tactlessly, i.e.
taking items from residents" (Scott *et.al.*, 2011: 265). Following an
incident the staff would avoid the person with dementia so there was an
absence of positive interaction, and tasks were done quickly thereby
deskilling the person, who could have done the task with support. The
person with dementia was excluded and outpaced (Kitwood, 1997). Scott
et al. (2011) recommend that staff receive specialist training in dementia
that includes communication skills, as well as opportunities to develop
understanding, compassion and empathy. In addition that guidelines and
support need to be provided to staff when confronted with aggression. An
important reflection point here is that most informal carers do not receive
any training in caring for someone with dementia or the management of
complex behaviour.

Carers' Belief Systems

Belief systems affect carers' capacity to sustain relationships with the cared for person. This is evidenced in a range of research studies such as that undertaken with 43 carers from the African American community in Chicago. Farran *et al.*, (2003) found that some carers had a 'personal spiritual philosophy' expressed as follows:

- 'I am too blessed to be stressed',
- 'This too will pass'
- 'You need a sense of humour. Without God and a sense of humour, care giving would be really too hard to do.'
- 'Anger only destroys you. Instead of "Why me?" I would have to ask "Why not me?" … We were married for 29 years – 26 without disease. Why should I be exempt from hard times?' (Farran *et al.*, 2003: 365-368).

These beliefs were underpinned and sustained by religious faith. The carers were actively engaged with their church that ministered to the black community. Farran *et al.* argue that as black churches in the USA have survived slavery, responded to discrimination and oppression, as well as provided life-long support, they are significant spiritually, socially and politically.

Stuckey (2003: 344) found that it is not necessary to have a spiritual faith, but rather a sense that "life is an ethical and moral journey" - a theme derived from interviewing 32 spouses where the partner had dementia. The beliefs that were significant to carers were the importance of people looking after each other during difficulties; the need to find some "meaning and purpose even amid pain and suffering" (p.350), and supporting the well-being of the person with dementia, as this was felt to be purposeful and morally right:

> If you cannot change something, if you can just stop struggling for a moment and be still and let it evolve, it might evolve into something really good for you. And I think [care giving] is the same thing … I can't see anything good coming out of this, but the simple fact of the matter is that I can't change it. So if I do my best within the context of it and stop struggling and really try to enjoy the time with him that I have, to the best of our abilities to enjoy it, then that's enough. And I will see what happens down the line … things have always been okay. I'm kind of a survivor (Female Agnostic Caregiver) (Stuckey, 2003: 345).

The above quote from a carer demonstrates a positive belief system, the ability to endure even when faced with extreme difficulties, as well as an acceptance and empathy towards the person with dementia. This was demonstrated by Susan in her thinking and behaviour after she was told by the Alzheimer's Society to: "walk over a bridge" into her mother's world. This was echoed by other carers who chose not to contradict the cared for person, but rather went with them to where they currently were recognising that the only change they had control over was how they responded to the person with dementia. Nick spoke of Simon thinking he was on holiday in North Africa, when in fact he was in hospital. Nick engaged with him in these conversations, which reassured him.

In the same way that the carers had been able to describe the enduring and positive aspects of their relationship with the person with dementia, they also identified what had been challenging, difficult and stressful, and the beliefs and resources they had been able to call upon. Theresa spoke in practical terms of how she organised and supported her parents until eventually they came to live with her. As her parents' health deteriorated she developed approaches to solve difficulties for herself and her parents, although she was finally providing nursing care and not getting more than four hours sleep a night. She explained:

> I think quite unconsciously the Karate and Tai Chi helped me to release the tension. Plus I have always been given a great sense of my own abilities by both parents. I have always been told that you set your mind to something and make a plan. I am a great problem solver, I have done it all my life in my career, and as consequence I treated each challenge as that, a problem to be solved.

The skills that Theresa had acquired in her professional life were transferred to her role as a carer and her approach was highly pragmatic. Ruth spoke of "absorbing a lot of the stress" when social care staff and family expressed concerns about her mother. Her approach to dealing with this was "to go and have a ciggie and a drink." Nick spoke of having a couple of glasses of wine and taking a Valium tablet. Ruth and Nick both stated that the stress was not emanating from the person with dementia but rather from family, health and social care services.

Angela found some of the ideas of Buddhism useful, such as impermanence, as a concept, and the importance of not becoming attached to difficult thoughts and feelings, but she did not use any spiritual practices. At one stage she sought counselling, which she found supportive. Elaine spoke of

Buddhism too and the importance for her of learning from her life experiences, and finding an "inner voice" that is able to connect with something greater linked to a common purpose. A primary source of strength was her belief in the concept of hope.

Nick identified his humanitarian values, as the motivation for him to care for Simon. He expressed uncertainty about his sense of any personalised God:

> in so far as I feel there is something special, and something that transcends and something very powerful, God is love. And that's the only way in which I can really explain being the best of me in my personal life. So that's really what it means, that's the thing that moves me and makes me want to do things, that's the best of me.

The concept of love as a factor that motivates and underpins humanitarian values, was also expressed by Susan, as she talked about her love, and the strength of character that her mother had given her. She spoke of the impact for her and her mother when she moved into her house to care for her:

> I think all the way through there was resentment, but also a lot of love and a lot of joy. But the worry that fell from mum's face, all the worry lines, she'd got a very lined face before just went away and she had her beautiful face back again.

Susan spoke of spiritual connections between the family in life and death, which gave her solace and a sense of continuity. What enabled her to cope as a carer was her compassion for others: "I think once you are a carer you always carry on caring, and you look for someone else to care for, it's a bit like a bug, you can't seem to get rid of it." This view was not expressed by any of the other carers.

As already stated Stuckley's (2003) research with 32 spouses where a partner had dementia, found that it was not necessary to have a spiritual faith, but it was important to live life with a commitment to help others when in difficulty, as well as being able to derive some meaning and understanding from the situation. The carers saw their engagement with the person with dementia as the morally right thing to do, and in cases where there had been a substantial emotional involvement based on deep affection such as for Susan, Theresa and Nick, this gave the caring its own momentum. However, for Angela, Ruth and Elaine the relationship was more complex and their motivation was partly due to their sense of family

obligation, which was stronger than their previous difficulties with their
mothers. For example Angela spoke of feeling coerced and emotionally
manipulated by her mother, who had cared for Angela in the past and now
expected this to be returned:

> she would put on the pressure of, 'well I took care of you when you were
> ill, now you should come and take care of me, that's what you have to do!'
> That's what she would say ... that's just what you do, that's what you do in
> families.

Angela had internalised the belief that family members are obligated to
each other and was resentful of her mother's expectations of her, but she
still expected her oldest child in the future to care for their sibling with
disabilities.

Analysis of Beliefs about Caring

In Chapter 2 the theory of Twigg and Atkin (1994) was introduced. They
identified three approaches to caring. Carers can demonstrate more than
one approach at the same time. The approaches with the resultant
behaviours are reproduced again in figure 5.1.

Figure 5-1: Approaches to Caring

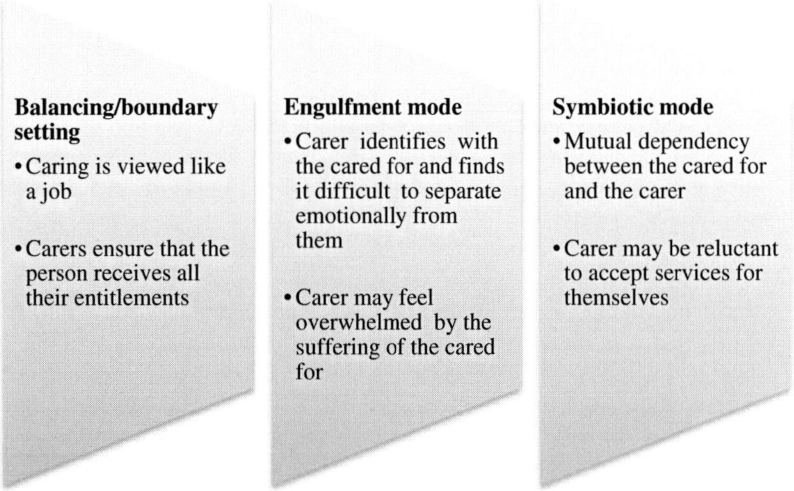

Balancing/boundary setting	Engulfment mode	Symbiotic mode
• Caring is viewed like a job	• Carer identifies with the cared for and finds it difficult to separate emotionally from them	• Mutual dependency between the cared for and the carer
• Carers ensure that the person receives all their entitlements	• Carer may feel overwhelmed by the suffering of the cared for	• Carer may be reluctant to accept services for themselves

(Adapted from Twigg and Atkin, 1994)

The balancing/boundary setting approach results in carers being informed about the cared for's health needs and entitlements. The carer develops a professional relationship with health and social staff. For example Nick advocated for Simon and suggested to his psychiatrist that he be discharged from hospital into a care home prior to the implementation of the NHS and Community Care Act 1990, as funding would be simpler. He arranged for him to attend a day centre, monitored his financial affairs with Social Services and purchased clothing for him. When Nick was undertaking these activities he was in the balancing/boundary setting mode; however there were times when Nick felt overwhelmed and found himself emotionally engulfed as a consequence of Simon's vulnerability especially when his caring role was rejected by the family:

> When they [Simon's family] were trying to take me away from Simon's care they were really in a sense removing the one person who has this shared history and could make things happen for Simon. Even when it came to conversation, I was able to talk to Simon because I knew the things that had been important to Simon. The things that he'd had enthusiasm about and was able to discover, the fragments in his memory of those things that were still left. Without that shared history, you know it's not just taking somebody, knocking somebody out looking at a piece of bureaucracy, you know watch our backs and get him out of the way. You know you are taking the core out of someone's life.

Nick as a gay man was able to share with Simon the cultural history of oppression and discrimination that gay people have experienced. They had both lived through a time when homosexuality was criminalised and categorised as a mental illness (Turnball, 2001). Nick's belief in love was the motivating force for his compassion and is evidenced in his behaviour towards Simon, and validates Kitwood's (1997) view that love should be an essential element of person centred care for people with dementia.

Ruth was motivated by her mother's request not to be moved into an institution, and by her belief that her knowledge of health and social care services would ensure that her mother could receive services that would enable her to stay at home with her quality of life maintained. Her approach falls within the balancing/boundary setting mode, and when she did experience feelings of engulfment these were caused by family and social care staff's concerns that her mother should be moved into a care home. Ruth co-ordinated the care her mother received from health and social care services.

Angela found her mother's demands increasingly difficult to manage. She expressed gratitude to the services that supported her, such as the Carers' Centre, day centre and care home. She was emotionally engulfed by the impact of her mother's behaviour on herself. Her engagement with her mother was based on a belief in family obligation in the same way as Ruth and Elaine.

Feelings of engulfment were also expressed by Elaine, but less in terms of her mother's illness and more about her own sense of loss. She stated a belief that families should look after each other, and felt guilty about her mother living in a care home.

Theresa received minimal support from health and social care services. Her approach was balancing/boundary setting which ensured that her parents would be able to remain living together. She had problem solving skills that were transferable from her career as a manager. Theresa undertook most of the personal and practical care of her parents.

Susan's approach to caring for her mother was motivated through her belief in the importance of love, which was articulated with the same strength of feeling as Nick for Simon. She ensured that the services her mother received were appropriate and met required quality standards, so in that sense she was balancing/ boundary setting. She felt engulfed when care services were delivered in a way that was disrespectful and demeaning to her mother.

The symbiotic mode between carers and the cared for where there was a mutual dependency was less evident, although there were many examples of an intuitive understanding by the carer of the person with dementia's needs. Susan for instance spoke of an observation a friend made to her that she was 'always able to second guess' what her mother wanted most of the time.

Carers' Support Systems

The carers were able to identify activities that they engaged with that provided diversion from the responsibilities of caring. Elaine watched television that was entertaining and played repetitive games. Angela found that studying and reading provided a mechanism for her to reduce her stress levels, but as her mother became more restless this became increasingly difficult to do. Nick enjoyed going to the cinema or having a meal out with his partner. Theresa's interest in Tai Chi became a regular activity. Susan found going into the garden provided an emotional release from the care of her mother.

Support at a personal level was important for all the carers. Susan stated that seeing how gentle her husband was with her mother and herself brought them back together, as they had been planning to separate. Ruth's partner provided practical support in cleaning her mother's house so that it was habitable again. In addition she enabled her to understand her mother better:

> She was very kind to my mother, she would say things to my mother that nobody had ever said to her, like she mattered or that she was a valuable person and such things ... So she kept me going because I started to understand my mother a bit better.

The carers were able to identify how they had developed as people through the experience of caring, and for some such as Ruth and Elaine it was the knowledge that they were prepared and able to support their mothers even though they had not received appropriate care as children. Nick and Susan identified that they had become more assertive and better able to "take people on." Nick had developed skills in writing in a manner that made bureaucratic organisations such as Local Authorities and the NHS take account of his concerns. Angela learnt to take care of herself so that she could care for others, while Elaine learnt the importance of communication and that caring has to be shared. Theresa explained that the experience of being a carer had made her grateful that she had been able to care for her parents so they could remain together.

> Grateful that I could do for them what I did, but sad that it has not changed significantly, because I know that we had the wherewithal to do certain things because of the jobs we'd had, we'd had good salaries for years, but also because of who I was. If you are not somebody who copes well with change, as a carer, then it's hellish. If you are not somebody who has the resources, I mean emotionally as well as financially to do what you like to do. Then the strain becomes doubled ... trebled. If you are somebody who is not a natural carer, then it should be okay to say so, and I don't think it is ... I think that I learned that caring is really not for everybody, but that I am glad that I did it.

Local Authority eligibility criteria to access an assessment for services for people with dementia and carers have become increasingly restrictive. Care services are means tested and there are difficulties in carers receiving high quality domiciliary care and respite care services (House of Commons,

2008). As the cared for person's dementia progressed health and social care services were increasingly needed, and it is the carers' experience of these services to which I now turn.

CHAPTER SIX

CARERS' ENCOUNTERS WITH HEALTH AND SOCIAL CARE SERVICES

Introduction

I have analysed the carers' experiences and views about health and social care services by adapting the Skills for Care (2010) 'Carers' Common Core Principles'. I have used these as a benchmark standard to compare and contrast the carers' lived experience against the recommended standard of good practice. The adapted principles are:

- Carers as equal partners in care
- Carers' capacity to continue with the caring role
- Support provided to carers to prevent ill health
- Carers' choices and involvement in decisions
- Quality of support provided to carers
- Support that carers receive as their role changes

The purpose of the principles is to ensure that carers are involved and engaged with by health and social care services in a manner that recognises their contribution to the cared for person. Furthermore, that the needs of carers for support in their own right are recognised. The carers' stories were assessed against these principles.

Carers as Equal Partners in Care

The expectation implicit in the principle that carers are equal partners in care is that the expertise of carers is acknowledged and validated; furthermore, their knowledge about how best to meet the needs of the person with dementia is sought. This expectation is underpinned by the social model, as opposed to the medical or individual model of disability (Oliver and Sapley, 2006). A key element of the medical model is that professional expertise is seen as dominant in the assessment and management of the person's care, irrespective of the person's views or that of the carer. An example of the medical model underpinning practice was given by Nick:

> I would go in there and they would say, 'we've had great trouble with Simon, now just listen to this, this morning we have washed all his clothes, we have ironed them and I gave him this pile of clothes and I told him go upstairs and put them in his chest of drawers.' Well Simon for a start didn't know where his room was in the house, he didn't know where he was, let alone where his chest of drawers was! So can you imagine the kind of tensions, and I obviously thought, well what can we do about this? I said to them, 'but he doesn't know where his room is.' And I tried to say as gently as possible, but they were really thinking that I was being over sympathetic to Simon and not understanding their problems.

Nick described feeling as if he were "walking on egg shells" with the staff, and although he sought the support of Simon's social worker, she appeared busy and disengaged. Nick's view was that the expectations that the care staff had of Simon were unrealistic and how they managed his care precipitated his violent outbursts. In the end a Community Psychiatric Nurse (CPN) advised the staff how to manage his behaviour and not to "corner him in any way." Although Nick had sought to act as an advocate for Simon in an attempt to ensure that his care was appropriate, the advice of the CPN had more credibility than that of the carer.

The importance of positive engagement with the person with dementia especially when they are being washed and dressed, so they understand what is happening and do not think they are being assaulted, is a basic requirement of dementia care (Morris and Morris, 2010). Susan's decision to move into her mother's home to care for her was as a result of an especially distressing incident where her mother had been left naked:

> what had happened was that the carers had come in and left mum with no clothes on, because she hit them. And my sister rang me to say that mum was sitting in the lounge with no clothes on, because she hit them ... And mum had started to hit out, and I did say to the carers, 'that mum will hit out if you keep trying to wash her in the living room with the net curtains, she can see out and the world she thinks can see in ... But if you always go how we've asked you to do it ... let her smell the soap, let her get her head around what she is doing, then she'll wash. But if you start to undress her then she will start to hit you because as far as she is concerned, you are just coming out of the blue, trying to take her clothes off! ... you'd have to reassure her and try to keep her modesty as best you could.

Susan explained that the most effective way to encourage her mother to do things was to dance with her. She would put the radio on and dance with her mother who then became relaxed and co-operative. Susan spoke of her mother getting a "bad reputation" as she would hit the transport men who came to take her to the day centre, but as Susan explained "if you are dozing in the chair and you wake up because you hear the key and two burly men come in you would." When Susan cared for her mother these incidents did not occur and she found it especially sad as the lack of person centred care, that is care that is tailored to meet individual needs and preferences, made a gentle person aggressive. This is a vivid example of Kitwood's (1997:45) "malignant social psychology" where the care practices are devoid of social interaction, emotional warmth and validation of the person's feelings.

The importance of knowing the person's personality and biography was further illustrated by Susan when she explained that her mother had been house proud and liked to have plastic flowers around the house. After the onset of dementia she would put "dolly mixture" sweets around the house, and she screwed paper up into balls and put them on the stairs. Susan knew that this was her mother making her home look attractive, whereas care staff thought she was untidy, and wrote this in the daily record kept in the house even when asked not to by Susan. A consistent factor for the carers was that the biography of the person with dementia was not routinely sought by health and social care staff. The person's life story and preferences in daily living routines and diet, which helped to explain their behaviour and enabled their needs to be sensitively met, were not obtained (Brooker, 2007). The care staff's task became more challenging and difficult, but more importantly the well-being of the person with dementia was adversely affected.

The carers were able to provide a limited number of examples where individual staff had engaged with them, as equal partners in the process of caring for the person with dementia. Theresa spoke of the occasion when she creatively used a sterile urinary catheter to keep her father's stoma open after he had pulled the tube out. This impressed the medical and nursing staff who found this inventive. Theresa received insufficient assistance with care tasks, in spite of both parents having complex nursing needs. She was provided with minimal training by nursing staff, for example in peg feeding.

Ruth found the last social worker involved with her mother to be supportive, as she reinforced Ruth's view to the care workers that complaints would not be made by her about her mother's poor hygiene if she refused to be assisted with washing. Ruth was clear about the services her mother needed and who should deliver them, especially after a private sector domiciliary care agency failed to visit her mother for several weeks due to staff sickness. Ruth insisted that the Local Authority's domiciliary care service support her mother:

> I think the social care people probably saw me, as a bit more, 'this is what I want, and this is what I'm having!' because I wasn't prepared to have what they'd offered her before, because I knew it won't work. So I had to put my foot down and be very firm.

Because she understood the workings of the health and social care system Ruth was able to advocate for her mother and ensure that practical services were provided, so that her mother was able to remain living in her own home. She commented that no one was co-ordinating her mother's care apart from herself.

Nick spoke of how he had given Simon baths in the care home. He was closely observed by the care staff, who recognised by this stage that they required his assistance if outbursts from Simon were to be avoided. In fact Nick provided training to staff as to how best to approach Simon.

> in those days you could smoke, so I used to give Simon a cigarette and some green grapes and tell him he was going to have a bath and he'd say, 'no no I had a bath this morning,' and I'd say, 'ah just come on with me.' And sometimes he would and sometimes he wouldn't, and so sometimes I would just lure him along showing him the grapes you see, and he'd follow me along the corridor, and we would get to the bathroom and then he'd sit down on the loo, and then I would gradually undress him, and give him a cigarette, and light the cigarette and say, 'come on very, very quickly, let's just have a very quick bath, just to please them,' and so then he'd have a bit of a bath.

The care staff watched outside the bathroom, until they felt confident enough to undertake this task. Nick suggested that the one male member of staff gave Simon a bath as he "was very kind, very patient" and so would avoid Simon being "manhandled and having his clothes pulled off." Both Nick and Susan suggested that health and social care staff should ask carers how best to undertake personal care tasks. Ruth commented "there is a need for training about how to give somebody an all over wash without humiliating them."

The carers stated that in the main health and social care staff did not ask them about the cared for person's daily routines, hobbies, interests, previous occupation, life story, and the best way to complete personal and practical care tasks.

Carer's Capacity to Continue with the Caring Role

The above Skills for Care (2010) principle requires that an assessment should be made about the capacity of carers to continue to care, so support can be provided. The carers felt in the main that their needs were not a concern for health and social care staff. There was a lack of curiosity about them. Theresa said:

> To be honest I could just as well have been a block of wood ... I don't mean to say that they were cruel or unkind ... I could have been a bug eyed man from Mars, as long as I was doing that and I was doing it to an acceptable level, just go away and do it, that was the impression I was given.

Ruth spoke of assumptions made by the first social worker who had assessed her mother under mental health legislation, and arranged for her admission to hospital.

> the social worker made comments to me about, 'oh you know this must have been a lovely family home?' There was definitely a whole thing of disapproval there; you know 'how could you have let your mother get herself into this state?' Without any understanding whatsoever of the dynamics of that relationship, and how she pushed everyone away, and how in fact it became impossible to continue a relationship with her.

These assumptions of family obligations were echoed by Elaine who had tried to explain the difficulties in her relationship with her mother to a member of the care home staff:

> she said, 'oh well my dear, it doesn't really matter what sort of relationship you've had with your mother really, because it is still your responsibility.' Hang on a minute; I am not sure it is and those were the bits that have really jarred me, because where was her responsibility when I was thirteen and she wasn't caring for me, where was her sense of responsibility? That does colour how I might see my sense of responsibility, I don't think that is irrelevant I think it's very relevant.

This member of staff's attitude concurs with cultural assumptions around the role of the family: "The idea that kin support is founded, in whole or in part, upon duty and obligation, implies that there 'is something special' about social relationships which we have with kin, which makes them distinctively different from all other relationships" (Finch, 1989: 212). This assumption can be challenged, for example Nick's commitment to Simon was not born of kinship. Many lesbian women and gay men do invest in friendships and social networks as they may not have children, and have experienced rejection from their families (Turnball, 2002).

Susan was employed as a social worker by the Local Authority where her mother lived; however, rather than a source of support she found this created particular stresses. Her colleagues were unable to maintain the boundaries between her professional and personal roles. She felt that her situation was known about in the office but little real support was provided:

> I think most people saw me as resilient, most people saw me as coping because that's the face you wear as a carer especially if you're scared, well actually the [domicilary care] agency has written bad things about your mum, your mum's been labelled as aggressive so you are a social worker so you should be managing it all a bit better, you've cracked up at work a few times, so maybe there is a question mark over your ability.

The experience of being a carer has informed Susan's social work practice. "I think I listen, and I can hear, there is listening and hearing isn't there? And I think I can hear what they're asking, and I can ask the questions ... what can I do?"

The time period when the carers were supporting the person with dementia varied, but they should all have been offered a carer's assessment. Susan was offered a carer's assessment, and Angela suspected that she might have been assessed. Theresa, Nick, Ruth and Elaine were not offered a carer's assessment, so their capacity or wishes to continue to care was not discussed with them.

Support Provided to Carers to Prevent Ill Health

Angela sought counselling for herself as a result of the emotional impact of caring for her mother. Susan spoke of her physical exhaustion:

> There were times when I was so tired in the morning and mum would wander into our room and it would be half past five, and it had taken her a little time to have gone off to sleep. You don't sleep well and you've always got one ear out in case she wants to go to the toilet or you need to

change her or something you know, or she's not sleeping or just walking around ... So half past five, six o'clock especially at the weekend when it was time to get up, I felt like it was trying to walk through not only treacle but like a straight jacket just trying to get out of bed and plod.

Theresa talked about only ever getting four hours of sleep a night. She had a baby alarm in her bedroom, and could hear her father if he became distressed in the night, and she would go through to him. There was a lack of understanding by health and social care services about the strain of caring. Theresa said:

All of these things are not considered as kind of an ongoing downward spiral for a carer ... you have to be at screaming point before you are given a break, and then having been given a break, you are somehow miraculously meant to be reborn to this new fresh, fit, eager for the next round new person, instead of which of course, what should be is regular breaks, established straight at the beginning and increased as developments happen in the disease.

As Simon was cared for in various institutions it was not the physical exhaustion of caring for him daily that affected Nick, but rather his own removal by the family and Social Services from any involvement in the management of Simon's care. Following a hospital admission the care home would not readmit Simon. He was placed on a long stay ward in a psychiatric hospital which Nick described as bleak. The difficulties in bathing Simon recurred. Nick explained:

And he was incontinent back and front and it would have been far easier, pretty unpleasant though, but far easier to let me wash him. And as it was he could see these people coming towards him with these gloves and everything, and he would start to shout, rant and rave, 'you are not touching me!' and they used to take him away physically. Whereas I think I could have persuaded him to have some kind of shower, gone into the shower room and put on a pair of trunks and everything and got wet myself and washed him. But they weren't allowed to do that, he used to shout and rant and swear, and then I could hear him in the shower room screaming with fear and with rage.

Nick found these incidents very distressing and left the ward returning when Simon had been bathed. Simon's fears could have been reduced and the delivery of personal care made much easier for the staff, if Nick had been allowed to be involved. Just as the emotional impact of hearing Simon's screams on Nick were not acknowledged by staff, neither was Susan's need for reassurance and comfort identified. She said:

> I needed someone just to hold my hand and say, 'don't be scared, it's alright.' But it wasn't there ... I just wanted the old Florence Nightingale, I wanted a nurse to sit with me and talk to me, I wanted them to be gentle with mum, I wanted them to treat her like a person that she was, right to the end.

These comments from carers demonstrate how important it is that health and social care staff understand the physical and emotional demands of caring. It tended to be particular staff rather than whole services that were singled out, as being sensitive and reassuring. These small acts of kindness were remembered and valued. Susan recalled:

> the occupational therapist was excellent. And I remember he used me and popped me in the hoist so my husband could practice with me, and it was a sheepskin and I was in the air, I felt so peaceful, I thought, 'I am so comfortable, just leave me here, everyone go and leave me in this hoist, no one can get me, I can't get down and I am safe up here!' Really weird, but I felt cocooned and I don't want anyone to talk to me anymore, yes the occupational therapist was brilliant.

Nick found the guidance and validation as a carer given by Simon's psychiatrist helpful. He was advised to read a particular book about dementia and ways of dealing with Simon's behaviour. He was told that the 'social medicine' he provided was benefiting Simon greatly.

Elaine stated that the social worker had insightfully articulated how she and her sister felt about her mother's dementia and their sense of losing her again as they had as children. The community psychiatric nurse was described as kind, but caused confusion by providing inaccurate advice. But Elaine went on to say:

> she is very sweet, lovely and she calls me darling and everything ... she's got just a sort of quiet, calm voice and when I've been upset on the phone, she says, 'alright darling, it's okay darling, don't worry', and I thought I'd be really irritated with it, but I wasn't!

Elaine was reassured and comforted. Ruth spoke of the staff on the ward when her mother had been hospitalised:

> They were actually lovely; they even let me take her cat in to visit her ... I'd arrive on time and I had been running around like a lunatic, doing all sorts of things, I am shifting furniture to a point where I couldn't cope anymore. And I got to the hospital and I just burst into tears, and they were really really caring towards me, and they would take me in and give me a cup of tea, and asked me how I was and all the rest of it.

An incident was recounted by Nick:

> there was a Hungarian woman, quite bent and quite old, and she shouldn't have been working at all, and obviously in handover time they got to know that the family wanted to cut me out. And I remember taking Simon out of the building on one occasion just to this little seating area outside, and she came across and said, 'I am finding this difficult to tell you,' she said, 'I know what's going on and I think it's quite terrible, you've known Simon as a friend all these years, and I think it's absolutely awful, awful and we all do.' And she just broke down in tears.

When Simon died the family removed his body and cleared his room prior to Nick getting to the hospital, without any word of where he had been taken:

> The staff said, 'what can we do for you?' And I said 'I don't think there's anything you can do for me really, you've done a great deal for Simon and all the rest of it. And they said, 'well at least we can make you a cup of tea,' and somehow the kind of pathos of that was great. And you know we sat there and drank tea, and that was a kind of sharing somehow at the end.

These small acts of concern were remembered and assumed an importance for the carers, as they were emotionally validating and demonstrated an understanding of their feelings.

One notable finding from the research was that carers were often asked to speak to the cared for if there had been incidences of problematic behaviour rather as if the person with dementia was a wayward child. Ruth and Susan were contacted by social care staff about their mother's behaviour. Susan talked about the care workers thinking that she should be able to get her "mum to behave." This is an example of "infantilization – treating a person very patronizingly... as an insensitive parent might treat a very young child" (Kitwood, 1997:46). On one occasion, Elaine contacted her mother on the telephone at 7.00pm at the care home. She was told that she could not speak to her as she had been "agitated" at 3.00pm. It was pointed out by Elaine this was some time ago and when her mother did come to the phone "she is all sweetness and light she can't remember what's happened five minutes ago let alone what happened an hour ago!"

Carers' Choices and Involvement in Decisions

As already stated the experience of carers suggests that individual staff from health and social care services did engage with them, but in terms of a whole systems approach to work collaboratively with carers this did not occur. Nolan *et al.* (2001) emphasise the importance of relationship-based care, which stresses the need for positive relationships for the person with dementia and the carer. Elaine remembered unexpectedly heartening conversations that brought a sense of support to her, for example when she spoke to a member of staff in the care home where her mother was having respite care:

> I had this long conversation with this one carer, and she was saying her father had died from dementia about a year ago, now sometimes I don't think that's appropriate and I don't think that's helpful because it can close people down. But actually how she used it was very helpful because we had a long conversation and kind of compared notes in some ways which was really helpful, so that was alright.

There were other examples where the carers felt that at an individual level they were provided with information, but the interviews revealed that often the person with dementia's care was uncoordinated. For example Ruth said:

> I was left to pull all the pieces together. She'd fallen down the stairs and the stairs were not great and after some discussion it was thought, 'yes she should be downstairs.' So I had to go and move her furniture around, buy her a new bed, and rearranging somebody's house to downstairs is really quite hard ... I also had the OT [occupational therapist] in so I had the sockets raised so she wouldn't fall doing them, and grab rails put in various places. I had the Careline come in and had various monitors put in the house, so heat and cold, very cold house that, and a mattress monitor, a pendant, a belt one ... basically I was left to do all that and also I insisted she was not coming out of hospital until they got in Local Authority health care [domiciliary care], I was not having agency [private sector domiciliary care] again. They had fallen to pieces, absolutely; she had been left for weeks on end with nobody coming in.

The need to co-ordinate services and the consequences of poor quality domiciliary care were experienced by Susan too. She was surprised by the response she received from the community nurse when asked to visit to check if her mother was getting a bed sore. She was told to take a photograph of her mother's buttocks and send it to the community nursing staff so they could make an assessment. Susan thought this undignified for both herself and for her mother, but was unable to complain, as she felt "frightened" that her complaining might exacerbate the situation.

Nick said that when Simon was admitted to the care home there was a care plan, but he was not asked to contribute to it, even though he knew Simon's life story and there was no other carer or family member actively involved.

> I was saying to them you see, 'how about this, how about that, does anyone sit down for example and talk to Simon at any time?' 'We've got a care plan' was always the answer, which otherwise means it's not your business, and I was saying to them, 'would it be helpful, because I know it's very difficult for him to engage in conversation with people, would it be helpful if I wrote down some questions and answers you will get, because then it will give you some kind of scenario, because then you can play this little drama daily and it will give you an opportunity to get to know Simon' and I said, 'also he doesn't know anyone's names, and to be honest I forget the names, could you wear name badges? That was a very prickly suggestion to make re the name badges, there was this idea and it's handed down that 'we know what Simon's needs are, we are the professionals.'

The staff difficulties caring for Simon would have been reduced if they had engaged with Nick, and made use of the information he held about him. For Nick as a carer his expertise and knowledge were not accessed, nor was there any understanding of Simon's sexuality. The care home was not "gay-friendly" (Lavin, 2008:57) and chose to ignore Simon and Nick's sexuality, conversely the day centre that Simon attended recognised this was part of Simon's identity. Simon's psychiatrist was keen for Nick to be involved. He reviewed Simon's medication at Nick's request and involved him in review meetings. In a medical report he wrote that he "could not speak too highly of the support given by Simon's devoted friend." Nick appreciated this recognition.

Angela found services provided by the voluntary sector and GP helpful, but from the social worker she received limited help as her mother had financial resources:

> there has to be some sort of difference in the way people behave towards people that have their own resources and people that don't have resources. I just didn't think it was fair, when I was phoning people they were saying, 'I just can't help you.' You ring them up and they just send you a manual and then that's it.

> They are not allowed to give any information about any of the care homes, and it's extremely frustrating and is very difficult so if there was some sort

of pool of information about what the care homes are like that would be really good.

Angela did say that the social worker had informally directed her to care homes, but had explained that they should not be doing this, as they could be seen to be promoting particular homes in a competitive market.

The Quality of Support Provided to Carers

The carers experienced a lack of curiosity about them from health and social care staff. This then impacted on the quality of support provided, although as already indicated individual professionals were validating of the carers. Theresa in her role as a volunteer with carers made a number of points about the importance of seeing people holistically:

> If social services and health care services professionals treat people as human beings and treat them in the round, then they are going to actually recognise that they have many more lesbians and gay, bisexual, transsexual and transgender people that they are dealing with on a daily basis ... They may ask the question of 'how long have you been looking after your friend?' Start your conversation so that you may lead to a point where you can actually ask, so, 'how long have you been living together, so do you think of yourselves as partners?'

Theresa went on to discuss health and social care staff feeling uncomfortable when talking about sex with carers whose partner had dementia. She pointed out that sexual violence on the part of the partner with dementia could occur. "It is a matter of getting things in the wrong order, foreplay gets lost somewhere. But nobody is talking about sex." This relates not only to the sexuality of people but their age too. Theresa commented it is "as though there is a cut off point for physical intimacy, it doesn't mean having sex, it can just be physical intimacy." This resonates with "old equals asexual" where culturally older people are assumed to have no interest in sexual relationships (Thompson, 2001: 90). Theresa explained:

> I have had nursing homes who separate two women just for holding hands on a sofa. Not just because the other residents are bothered by it or even the nursing staff may not be bothered by it. But because Mrs Smith's family doesn't like the fact that Mrs Smith holds hands with Miss Jones, because Mrs Smith has got a family, so she can't be like that. Well catch a clue, maybe she was always like that but in her younger years she was kind of expected to get married, but maybe Mrs Smith was always like that, maybe she wasn't, it doesn't matter. The fact is that Mrs Smith gets a great

deal of comfort and emotional support from holding hands with Miss Jones. What's wrong with that?

The above characterises care that is not supporting the needs of residents but rather the expectations of their families, as if dementia precludes people from making choices about their relationships. Nick was surprised that the Local Authority with responsibility for Simon's care was unable to provide any sign posting or information about services for lesbian women and gay men. He recalled an allegiance based on a shared sexuality that developed in the hospital where Simon died:

> There was one guy who was very blunt, a real 'Bill Sykes' kind of character, very difficult, and when I went there first of all, very brusque, quite aggressive, in even answering the simplest question. And then he got to know that Simon was gay, he'd obviously been to the handover meetings, and he got to know I was gay and was just so kind, he was gay himself.

This is a positive example of the belief that "they can look after their own" (Smith and Clavert, 2001:8-12); moreover it demonstrates solidarity and a sense of community in a bleak institutional hospital environment.

Support that Carers Receive as Their Role Changes

In none of the carers' accounts was there any indication of a systematic process implemented by health and social care services in supporting carers to manage the transitions precipitated by the illness, but there were examples of individual staff offering support. Susan spoke of the kindness of a nurse in the final weeks of her mother's life who explained what to expect. Nick related the incident of staff on the ward giving him a cup of tea after Simon died. The focus of health and social care staff was on caring for the person with dementia rather than engaging with their carers too. Once the person with dementia died health and social care services withdrew.

In Chapter 2, I reproduced the trajectory of caring that was developed by Tanner and Harris (2008). To re-cap, health and social care services view the carer initially as resource providing care; as the needs of the person increase they become a co-worker. Clearly the pressures of caring can become overwhelming for carers such that they are in need of services themselves. Finally health and social care services assume responsibility for the person with dementia as the complexity of their needs increase. This process was not as simple or continuous for the carers I interviewed.

As a consequence I have amended Tanner and Harris's model to show their experiences against this cyclical process in figure 6.1. When services were provided this was to support the person with dementia rather than assist carers sustain a life away from caring. Once the person with dementia was in care or had died services such as bereavement counselling were not offered.

Figure 6-1: Caring at Different Stages

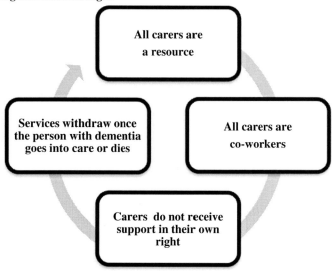

(Adapted from Tanner and Harris, 2008:178)

Ruth spoke of having to provide support to the carer who was present when her mother died rather than receiving any support herself: "I said to this carer at the time, what a fantastic gift she had given my mother to actually be with her when she died." Ruth suggested that there should be training to support carers with managing end of life care.

Simon's family removed his body from the hospital and did not advise Nick of any funeral arrangements or invite him to the memorial service. He found these actions personally rejecting and unkind. Three and half years later the family placed Simon's name on the family gravestone, prompted by correspondence from Nick: "they'd airbrushed him out of their lives and they'd airbrushed after death, and not even giving him a funeral which was attended by people he knew, or people who were nearest to him."

Bereavement is an emotionally difficult time. Generally other people are sympathetic but for lesbian women and gay men this may not be the case (Hicks, 2008). It could be argued that given the difficulties that Nick had experienced with Simon's family because of their homophobia a particular responsibility lay with health and social care services to have offered some information and advice about bereavement services that he could have accessed. However, Nick like the other carers had no expectations about being supported to manage change for either themselves, or the person for whom they cared.

Managing Transitions

Hellström *et al*'s (2007) research on how changes are experienced in relationships was discussed in Chapter 2. To state again briefly it comprises three phrases that carers' experience with the cared for. During the first phase of the model; "sustaining couplehood" people try to maintain the relationship. If there had been difficulties in the relationship between the cared for and carer prior to the onset of the illness, plans can be made supported by health and social services, to meet anticipated needs. Such an approach would have been useful to Ruth and Elaine, as they both had had a difficult relationship with their mother prior to the onset of dementia. Susan, Nick and Theresa spoke of the approaches that they used to maintain their relationship with the cared for throughout the illness with an emphasis on positive activities to circumvent difficulties.

In the second phase, "maintaining involvement", there is a growing realisation of the changes that the dementia is causing to the cared for person. Susan and Theresa were able to recount instances of their physical exhaustion and Angela spoke about her mother's need for attention. In the third phase, 'moving on', the carers' sense of their identity changes and they start to re-evaluate their life without the responsibility for the person with dementia. One consistent factor for all the carers was a sense of satisfaction that they had maintained their relationship with the person throughout the illness. This was a comfort to them if the person was no longer with them.

Notwithstanding this the analysis of the carers' experiences against the Skills for Care (2010) 'Carers' Common Core Principles', has demonstrated that the delivery of health and social care services, has in the main, not been informed by these principles.

Summary

This chapter analysed and discussed the findings following the interviews with six carers that explored the experience of caring, coping approaches, and carers' encounters with health and social care services. The findings indicated similarities of experience between the carers that developed into themes. The final part of the analysis adapted the Skills for Care (2010) 'Carers' Common Core Principles.' This acted as an evaluative measure as the principles were compared against the experience of the carers. The importance of previous emotional ties and an understanding of the person's life story, preferences and needs, as well as their personality emerged as paramount in ensuring good quality care for the person with dementia. The dominant model of care provided by health and social care services that emerges from the carers' stories is a task orientated approach within the medical model. The unique needs of the person with dementia and their carer were often disregarded with the result that the delivery of some services was of poor quality. Consequently, carers experienced stress and anxiety, and in some cases had to proactively manage the care of the person. There was a consistent lack of interest or curiosity about the needs of carers by health and social care staff, who made assumptions about the carers' ability to continue to care. These issues are explored in the messages for practice in Chapter 7.

CHAPTER SEVEN

MESSAGES FOR PRACTICE

Introduction

This book has been written following research that centred on the lived experience of six carers of people with dementia: five women and one man, three identified as lesbian or gay. They were informal unpaid carers. Five carers were or had been caring for their mother, and one cared for a friend. The carers had all retained a relationship with the cared for person throughout the duration of the illness. I have set their experiences within a legislative and policy context as well as using theory as a means to make sense of their roles and identities as carers. Furthermore I have drawn on other research findings. Key to the approach taken has been to ensure that the person with dementia is central to the discussions with carers. In this concluding chapter I draw together messages for practice that would enhance the lives of the people with dementia and carers.

The Experience of Caring

The motivation for caring among participants varied along a continuum of strong emotional bonds to a sense of obligation towards the cared for, that was linked to the concept of hierarchy in family relationships based on familial ties rather than affection. This echoed Finch's (1989) research with health and social care services responding to this hierarchy in relationships too. Conversely, families were able to curtail and control support where the carer was not family. This was evident in the relationship between the two friends, Nick and Simon. As the illness progressed, changes occurred in how Nick (the carer) related to Simon. Some carers lost the emotional support the cared for person had provided before the illness, and found their relationship was reversed, with this person now dependent on them. For one carer the fear which her mother had instilled evaporated, and she suddenly saw her mother as frail and vulnerable. An anxiety the carers expressed was that the person with dementia would cease to recognise them. The "horror" of not being remembered, as expressed by Ruth, indicates how identities between the carer and cared for are bound up with each other (as discussed by Morris and Morris, 2010). Most of the carers adjusted to these changes, as evidenced by their continued affection for the person with dementia, without dwelling on regrets for the person lost. Social isolation is often an issue for people with dementia, and this became the case with some carers too as they had less time for friends and family due to their caring responsibilities. The enduring and positive aspects of the carers' relationship with the person with dementia focused on shared humour, as well as supporting the cared for to enjoy favourite activities.

Coping Approaches

The carers adopted a number of short and longer term approaches enabling them to cope, such as having a drink or cigarette; going into the garden and thereby removing themselves; seeing a counsellor, or developing plans in response to problems. The motivation to continue to care varied among the carers; key drivers appeared to be love for the cared for person, and family obligation. Using the work of Twigg and Atkins (1994: 122) I was able to theorise the carers' attitude to their role, identifying the "boundary setting" mode where the carer develops knowledge and skills enabling them to behave as a professional in their caring role, and "engulfment" mode, where the carer is overwhelmed by the needs of the cared for person. Four of the carers presented as boundary setting most of the time, while two talked of feelings of engulfment, intertwined with boundary setting. The carers identified a range of simple activities and significant relationships that had given them pleasure and support. The carers reported that the act of caring had made them more assertive, knowledgeable, and had enhanced their self-esteem and self-reliance, while one carer spoke of her gratitude for being able to care, so that she could keep her parents living together.

Carers' Encounters with Health and Social Care Services

There were consistencies in the experiences the carers had of health and social care services. They were generally not treated as equal partners in the caring process; moreover the biography of the cared for person was not sought, and the carers' views and advice were not considered. They were not routinely involved in the development of care plans. This led to instances of poor quality care, particularly around bathing, which were abusive in the case of Simon and Susan's mother. Carers found that care was not co-ordinated by one professional and services were fragmented. Care practice was underpinned by the medical model of care; so the focus of intervention was on the dementia, without a holistic assessment of the person's needs or story.

There was generally felt to be a lack of interest in the person with dementia and their carer among professionals. Consequently Simon's sexuality was not perceived as significant even when his family imposed constraints on Nick's contact. This was not challenged by Social Services despite Nick's feeling that there were elements of homophobia at play. Carers told of expectations that they would continue to care, without professionals checking whether they required further support. There was an underlying assumption that the carers who were daughters had filial responsibilities, irrespective of the history of the relationship which was never sought anyway. Two carers were asked to speak to the cared for about their behaviour, as if they were misbehaving children, which demonstrates ignorance about the nature of the illness.

Only one of the six carers had definitely been offered a carer's assessment, their legal entitlement (Department of Health, 1995; Department of Health, 2005; Department of Health 2008a). On the whole, the carers' experience contradicted both the spirit and aims of legislation and social policy, which are for health and social care services to work with carers as equal partners by valuing their expertise, and recognising their need for support. There were instances when individual professionals were compassionate in spite of the overall system being disjointed.

Images as Metaphors of the Caring Role

When I had analysed the interview data the images below came to my mind as representations of my view of the carers in their caring role, and equally my progress as a researcher where the process enabled my understanding to change and develop. These simple and sometimes humorous pictures convey particular meanings to me beyond the data portrayed in the literal form.

Figure 7-1: Nick in the Role of Carer

This image made me think of Nick caring for his friend Simon when I recalled how he would take Simon out to his favourite haunts from the care home or hospital. Nick spoke with such pleasure about these outings. I felt that Nick knew Simon so well that he was able to provide him with a range of positive experiences and was empathetic to his needs. What is more even though Simon's dementia had changed their friendship it had not diminished it.

Figure 7-2: Ruth in the Role of Carer

The image of Nick and Simon contrasted quite sharply with how I saw Ruth, as I perceived her as very effectively organising and co-ordinating her mother's care. She felt that support from health and social care services was very variable and ultimately she had to take control. When I reflected on this it was clear she was often more knowledgeable about what was available than the health and social care staff, and had to inform them about resources. I could see that they would respond to her as if she was in charge.

Figure 7-3: Theresa in the Role of Carer

Theresa struck me as very resourceful and resilient. She was caring for her mother and father when she was in her thirties. Her response to problems was to develop a plan, and often she came up with creative ideas to best meet her parents' needs. I saw her as a practical and capable person, who always found a way through, and managed to keep her parents together with her throughout the duration of the illness.

Figure 7-4: Elaine in the Role of Carer

I saw Elaine as cast down by the weight of her history with her mother. Her sense of being abandoned as a teenager by her felt very alive and present. The interview seemed like a circle that kept returning to Elaine's hurt and confusion. It was rather like someone talking about an unrequited love, and constantly wondering what went wrong without being able to accept the situation, and the fact that maybe she never would know the reasons. It was perpetual grief, and this was the image that came into my mind. I felt intensely sad for Elaine as she was clearly a very caring person, and was doing all she could now to support her mother.

Figure 7-5: Angela in the Role of Carer

Angela seemed at times reluctant to give very full answers to questions. She would then suddenly change from being repressed in her responses to making very passionate statements that were unexpected. Underlying her reticence I felt that there was considerable frustration and anger, which in part had been ameliorated by her mother's admission to a care home.

Figure 7-6: Susan in the Role of Carer

Susan like Ruth had arranged much of her mother's care, but unlike Ruth she had also provided most of the personal care. Essentially I felt that Susan's caring for her mother had been rewarding to her, and was an expression of her love. I had a sense that she had enabled other people to support her, and her mother too, such as her husband. In addition to this she was able to work collaboratively with people without telling them what to do rather leading them, hence this cheerful picture of a group being led by Susan where everyone is moving forward in the same direction.

Figure 7-7: The Objective Researcher

This image is of me as the researcher when I first began the process. I was distant and impersonal and assumed that this would be me researching other people and coming to a series of conclusions. I was engaged at a cognitive and action level, but not emotionally. As I became more reflexive that changed in a process similar to that documented by Waines (2004). I realised how much the experience of the carers was prompting quite profound philosophical thoughts about the connection between personal values and choices that the carers had made, as well as the stories they told me about what the person with dementia had given to them.

Figure 7-8: The Reflexive Researcher

This final image came to represent me in terms of the dog being sheltered by the person (carer) with the umbrella. I felt that particular carers had shared their wisdom, and demonstrated such humanity that I learnt something about the importance of relationships during stormy times, and how values inform our actions. Their approaches to coping symbolised by the umbrella enabled them to keep the person with dementia safe, while they remained protected against the rain. I have learnt from them, and I am grateful for this new knowledge just as the dog is enjoying the social interaction while remaining dry. Furthermore becoming a researcher has given me confidence and a wish to share my understanding and knowledge with others. In summation, I feel that the research process and relationships that I have developed have given me so much in both a personal and professional capacity. I am keen to share what I have learnt with other people with the aim of enhancing the well-being of both people with dementia and carers.

Messages for Practice

There were some striking similarities between the carers in their experiences and themes did emerge notwithstanding that they were caring at different periods of time and lived in various regions in the UK. I start with the legislative and policy narrative of caring, and contrast this to the actual lived experience of caring.

The concept of carer was recognised and enshrined in law and social policy beginning with the Carers (Recognition and Services) Act 1995. This has been complemented by additional legislation and social policy supported by research. Carers' entitlements include support that enables them to gain employment, education and access leisure activities. Fundamental to this is the right to have their needs assessed. In spite of these legal entitlements the actual experience of caring is very different. What emerged from the carers' stories is a disjuncture between legislation, policy and practice. Further research could discover whether health and social care staff are simply unaware of the legislation and policy in relation to carers, or they assume that assessing carers' needs has a limited impact due to financial and resource constraints. Carers' assessments give the carer the opportunity to explain their needs, and be advised about financial benefits and resources. The act of being listened to as a carer can reduce feelings of isolation and gives opportunities for problem solving; equally it enables the carer to advise professionals about the needs of the person with dementia.

Person Centred Practice

Sanderson *et al.* (2008: 50) describe person centred thinking as identifying what is *important to* the cared for person, as well as what is *important for* the person. The latter often dominates, resulting in services that only meet people's physical needs with an emphasis on assessing risks, but fail to take account of the personal preferences of the cared for. In the carers' stories there were examples of health and social care staff not taking the advice of carers resulting in abusive practice; for example Susan's mother was left naked by domiciliary care workers as they could not wash her, even though they had been advised by Susan of an approach that worked, and of what was *important to her.*

There are opportunities for innovative changes to be made through the personalisation of services that enable carers to receive funding to employ and manage personal assistants, but equally there are concerns that funding may not be adequate to ensure sufficient care of the required quality, especially as the government has no plans at present to regulate personal assistants (Gardner, 2011). Notwithstanding this, there are practical approaches that support person centred thinking and planning that could be successfully used for people with dementia and carers. For example, simply recording what works and what does not work in how care is delivered to the person would have prevented the repetition of poor and abusive care practices highlighted by carers. Services were not gay friendly and indeed displayed a lack of interest or curiosity in the intimate networks of either the cared for or the carer. Consequently, the most pressing message to emerge from the research was the need for person centred thinking and practice to become embedded within the leadership, management and delivery of services.

Conclusion

Much of the practice experienced by carers interviewed for this study was founded on a medical model of intervention focusing on the dementia of the cared for. In spite of this the carers interviewed showed resilience and commitment. They advocated and safeguarded the person; moreover most of the carers derived continuing pleasure from their relationship. They all identified increased self-esteem because they had supported the person throughout the illness. I learnt through hearing the carers' stories how emotional bonds between people endure; people with dementia show us what it is that we all need - love, acceptance and the capacity to enjoy the moment. The loudest message for research and practice is that person centred thinking needs to be at the very heart of how we engage with people with dementia and their carers.

BIBLIOGRAPHY

Alzheimer's Society (2010) *Statistics.*
    http:/alzheimers.org.uk/scripts/documents [accessed: 5/1/2011]
Archibald, C. (2006) Gay and lesbian issues: learning on the (research)
    job, *The Journal of Dementia Care,* 14 (4): 21-23
Askham, J., Briggs, K., Norman, I., & Redfern, S. (2007) Care at home for
    people with dementia: as a total institution? *Ageing and Society,* 27: 3-
    24
Atkinson, R. (1998) *The Life Story Interview.* Thousand Oaks, California:
    Sage publications
Ballenger, J. (2008) Reframing dementia: the policy implications of
    changing concepts, in M. Downs & B. Bowers (eds) *Excellence in
    Dementia Care.* Berkshire: Open University Press, pp. 492-509
Bamford, C. (2000) Defining the outcomes of community care: the
    perspectives of older people with dementia and their carers, *Ageing
    and Society,* 20: 543-570
Banerjee, S. (2009) *Prescribing of Anti-Psychotic Drugs to People with
    Dementia.* London: Department of Health
Beck, J.S. (1995) *Cognitive Therapy.* New York: The Guildford Press
Becker, S. (2008) Informal family carers, in: K. Wilson, G. Ruch, M.
    Lymbery, A. Cooper (eds), *Social Work.* Harlow: Pearson Education,
    pp. 431-460
Beresford, P. (2005) Theory and practice of user involvement in research,
    in: L. Lowes & I. Hulatt (eds), *Involving Service Users in Health and
    Social Care Research.* Oxfordshire: Routledge, pp. 6-17
Bingley, A.F., Thomas, C., Brown, J., Reeve, J. & Payne, S. (2008)
    Developing narrative research in supportive and palliative care: the
    focus on illness narratives, *Palliative Medicine,* 22: 653-658
Blakemore, K. and Boneham, M. (1994) *Age, Race and Ethnicity.*
    Buckingham: Open University Press
Bochel, H., Bochel, C., Page, R. & Sykes, R. (eds) (2009) *Social Policy*
    (2nd ed). Harlow: Pearson Longman
Bolton, G. (2001) *Reflective Practice.* London: Paul Chapman Publishing
    Ltd
Braye, S. & Preston-Shoot, M. (1995) *Empowering Practice in Social
    Care.* Buckingham: Open University

Briggs, C.L. (2003) Interviewing, power/ knowledge and social inequality, in: J.F. Gubrium & J.A. Holstein. *Postmodern Interviewing,* California: Sage. pp. 243-254

British Sociological Association (2004) *Statement of ethical practice for the British Sociological Association.*
http:/www.britsoc.co.uk/equality/statement+Ethical+Practice
[accessed: 3/7/10]

Brooker, D. (2007) *Person-Centred Dementia Care.* London: Jessica Kingsley Publishers

Brown Cosis, H. (1998) *Social Work and Sexuality.* Basingstoke: Macmillan

Bruce, E. (1999) Holding on to the story: older people, narrative, and dementia, in G. Roberts, & J. Holmes (eds.) (1999). *Healing Stories.* Oxford: Oxford University Press

Bryden, C. (2005) *Dancing with Dementia.* London: Jessica Kingsley Publishers

Burton, M. (2008) Grounded constructions of carers: exploring the experiences of carers through a grounded approach, *British Journal of Social Work*, 38: 493-506

Butler, J. (1993) Bodies that matter. On the discursive limits of sex, in: R. Ward, A. Vass, C.Garfield, B. Cybyk (eds) (2005) A kiss is still a kiss? *Dementia,* 4 (1): 49-72

Bytheway, B. & Johnston, J. (1998) The social construction of 'carers', in: A. Symonds, & A. Kelly (eds) (1998) *The Social Construction of Community Care.* Basingstoke: Macmillan. pp. 241-262.

Canda, E.R. (2009) Chronic illness and transilience along my spiritual path, in D. Saleebey (ed) *The Strengths Perspective in Social Work,* (5th ed). USA: Pearson, pp. 72-92

Carers UK, (2009) *Profile of Caring.* http:/carersuk.org [accessed 9/2/09]

Cass, E., Robbins, D., Richardson, A. (2008) *Dignity in Care,* London: Social Care Institute for Excellence

Chelsa, M., Martusan, I., & Muwases, M. (1994) Continuities and discontinuities in family members' relationships with Alzheimer's patients. *Family Relations,* 43 (1): 3 -9

Cheston, R. and Bender, M. (1999) *Understanding Dementia.* London: Jessica Kingsley

Chung, P.Y.F., Ellis-Hill, C. & Coleman, P.G. (2008) Carers perspectives on the activity patterns of people with dementia, *Dementia,* 7(3): 359-381

Clark, A. & Emmel, N. (2010) *Using walking interviews.*
http:/manchester.ac.uk/realitiestoolkit#13. [accessed: 10/5/11]

Clarke, G. (1996) Conforming and contesting with (a) difference: how lesbian students and teachers manage their identities, *International Studies in Sociology of Education,* 2: 191-2009

—. (1998) Voices from the margins: regulation and resistance in the lives of lesbian teachers', in: M. Erben (ed) *Biography and Education A Reader,* London: Falmer Press, pp. 59-71

Cohen, L., Manion, L. & Morrison, K. (2007) *Research Methods in Education.* (6th edition). Oxford: Routledge

Coles, B. & Short, A. (2008) Families leading person centred planning, in: J. Thompson, J. Kilbane & H. Sanderson (eds), *Person Centred Practice for Professionals.* Berkshire: Open University, pp.231- 256

Commission for Social Care Inspection (2008a) *See me, not just the dementia.* London: Commission for Social Care Inspection

—. (2008b) *Putting People First: Equality and Diversity Matters.* London: Commission for Social Care Inspection

Concannon, L. (2009) Developing inclusive health and social care policies for older LGBT citizens. *British Journal of Social Work,* 39: 403-417

Couser Thomas, G. (2006) Disability, life narratives and representation, in: Lennard J. Davis (ed) *The Disability Studies Reader* (2nd ed).New York: Routledge, pp.399-401

Crepaz-Keay, D. (2006) Service user involvement in mental health services: what's the point? in: C. Jackson, & K. Hill, (eds). *Mental Health Today.* Brighton: Pavilion

Cummings, E and Henry, W. (1961) *Growing Old: The Process of Disengagement.* New York: Basic Books.

Dalley, G. (1987) *Ideologies of Caring – Rethinking Community and Collectivism.* Basingstoke: Macmillan

Dalrymple, J & Burke, B (2006) *Anti-Oppressive Practice Social Care and the Law.* Berkshire: Open University Press.

Davies, S. & Nolan, M. (2008) Attending to relationships in dementia care, in: M. Downs & B. Bowers (eds) *Excellence in Dementia Care.* Berkshire: Open University Press, pp.438-455

Department of Health (1990) *National Health Service and Community Care Act.* London: HMSO

—. (1995) *Carers (Recognition and Services) Act.* London: The Stationary Office.

—. (2000) *National Service Framework Older People.* London: The Stationary Office.

—. (2005a) Carers (Equal Opportunities) Act 2005. London: The Stationary Office

—. (2005b) Mental Capacity Act 2005. London: Stationary Office

—. (2006) *Our Health, Our Care, Our Say.* London: The Stationary Office
Department of Communities and the Local Government (2007) *Guidance on New Measures to Outlaw Discrimination on Grounds of Sexual Orientation in the Provision of Goods, Facilities and Services.* London: Department for Communities and Local Government
Department of Health (2008a) Carers at the Heart of the 21st Century Strategy. London: The Stationary Office
—. (2008b) *Putting People First.* London: The Stationary Office.
—. (2009) *National Dementia Strategy.* London: The Stationary Office.
—. (2010a) *Quality outcomes for people with dementia: building on the work of the National Dementia Strategy.* London: The Stationary Office
—. (2010b) *A Vision for Adult Social Care: Capable Communities and Active Citizens.* London: The Stationary Office
—. (2010c) *Carers and personalisation: improving outcomes.* London: The Stationary Office
Denscombe, M. (1998)*The Good Research Guide.* Buckingham: Open University Press
Denzin, N.K. (1989) *Interpretive Biography.* California: Sage
Dewaele, A., Cox, N., Berghe den Van, W. & Vincke, J. (2011) Families of choice? Exploring the supportive networks of lesbians, gay men and bisexuals, *Journal of Applied Social Psychology,* 41(2): 312-331
Dick, S. (2009) *Homophobic hate crime and hate incidents.* Manchester: Equality and Human Rights Commission
Dixey, R. (2010) Walking on thin ice, in L.Whitman (ed), *Telling Tales about Dementia.* London: Jessica Kingsley, pp. 45-51.
Doherty, D., Benbow, S.M., Craig, J. & Smith, C. (2009) Patients' and carers' journeys through older people's mental health services: powerful tools for learning, *Dementia,* 8 (4): 501-513
Drummond, M. (2006) Ageing gay men's bodies, *Gay and Lesbian Issues and Psychology Review,* 2(2): 44-59
Duvall, J. & Béres, L. (2007) 'Movements of identities: a map for therapeutic conversations about trauma', in: C.Brown & T. Augusta-Scott, (eds) (2007) *Narrative Therapy.* California: Sage, pp.229-250.
Egan, G. (2010) *The Skilled Helper,* (9th ed). Belmont, USA: Brooks/Cole Cengage Learning
Ellison, G. & Gunstone, B. (2009) *Sexual orientation explored: A study of identity, attraction, behaviour and attitudes in 2009.* Manchester: Equality and Human Rights Commission
Employment Equality (Sexual Orientation) Regulations 2003, London: The Stationary Office

Equality and Human Rights Commission (2009) *Beyond tolerance: making sexual orientation a public matter.* London: EHRC

Erben, M (1998) Biography and research method, in M. Erben (ed.) *Biography and Education: A Reader.* London: Falmer Press, pp. 4-17.

Erikson, E (1977) *Childhood and Society.* London: Paladin

Etherington, K. (2004) *Becoming a Reflexive Researcher.* London: Jessica Kingsley

Fannin, A., Fenge, L., Hicks, C., Lavin, N., & Brown, K. (2008) *Social Work Practice with Older Lesbians and Gay Men.* Exeter: Learning Matters

Farran, C.J., Paun, O, Elliott, M.H. (2003) Spirituality in multicultural caregivers of persons with dementia. *Dementia,* 2 (3): 353 -377

Finch, J. and Groves, D. (1983) *A Labour of Love.* London: Routledge & Kegan Paul

Finch, J. (1984) *Education as Social Policy.* London: Longmans

—. (1989) *Family Obligation and Social Change.* Cambridge: Polity Press

Fook, J. (2002) *Social Work: Critical Theory and Practice.* London: Sage

Frank, A.W. (1995) *The Wounded Storyteller: Body, Illness and Ethics.* Chicago: The University of Chicago Press

Gaine, C. (2010) Sexual orientation, in C. Gaine (ed) (2010) *Equality and Diversity in Social Work Practice.* Exeter: Learning Matters, pp.29-42.

Galpin, D. & Bates, N. (2009) *Social Work Practice with Adults.* Exeter: Learning Matters

Gardner, A. (2011) *Personalisation in Social Work.* Exeter: Learning Matters

Gardner, C. (2009) A carer's life: Is it Tuesday or Wednesday fortnight?, *Auto/Biography Yearbook*, 2009: 125-142

Gay Liberation Front Manifesto 1979, London: Gay Liberation Front Information Service

Gearing, D. & Dant. T.(1990) Doing biographical research, S.M. Pearce (1990) (ed) *Researching Social Gerontology, Concepts, Methods and Issues.* London: Sage, pp.143-159

General Social Care Council (2010) *Codes of Practice for Social Care Workers.* http:/ gscc.org.uk [accessed: 3/7/10]

Gibbs, G. (2007) *Analyzing Qualitative Data.* London: Sage

Gilligan, C. (1982) *In a Different Voice: Psychological theory and women's development.* Cambridge, Mass: Harvard University Press

Goffman, E. (1961) *Asylums.* London: Penguin

—. (1963) *Stigma.* London: Penguin

Golightley, M (2008) *Social Work and Mental Health* (3rd ed). Exeter: Learning Matters

Gorman, H. and Postle, K. (2003) *Transforming Community Care: A Distorted Vision.* UK: Venture Press

Graham, M (2007) *Black Issues in Social Work and Social Care.* Bristol: The Policy Press

Grant, G. (2003) Caring families, their support and empowerment, in K. Stalker, (ed) (2003) *Reconceptualising Work with Carers.* London: Jessica Kingsley, pp.96-116.

Griffiths, M. (1998) *Educational Research for Social Justice.* Buckingham: Open University Press

Hanmer, J. & Statham, D. (1988) *Women and Social Work.* Basingstoke: Macmillan

Harrison, J. (2006) Coming out ready or not! Gay, lesbian, bisexual, transgender and intersex ageing and aged care in Australia: Reflections, contemporary developments and the road ahead, *Gay and Lesbian Issues and Psychology Review,* 2(2):44-53

Hellström, I., Nolan, M., & Lundh, U. (2007) Sustaining 'couplehood', *Dementia,* 6 (3): 383 -409

Hicks, C. (2008) Looking forward: developing creativity in practice, in: A.Fannin, L. Fenge, C. Hicks, N. Lavin, K. Brown (2008) *Social Work Practice with Older Lesbians and Gay Men.* Exeter: Learning Matters, pp.66-75

HM Government (2010) *Recognised, valued and supported: Next steps for the Carers Strategy.* http:/dh.gov.uk/publications [accessed: 31/1/11]

Home Office (1998) Data Protection Act 1998. London: The Stationary Office

House of Commons Committee of Public Account (2008) *Improving services and support for people with dementia.* http:/publications.parliament.uk./pa/cm200708/cmselect/cmpubacc/22 8/228.pdf [accessed: 2/3/10]

Howe, D. (2009) *A Brief Introduction to Social Work Theory.* Basingstoke: Palgrave

Hughes, M. (2006) Queer ageing, *Gay and Lesbian Issues and Psychology Review,* 2(2): 44-59

Hunt, R., Cowan, K. & Chamberlain, B. (2007) *Being the gay one: experiences of lesbian, gay and bisexual people working in the health and social care sector.* London: Stonewall

Hunt, R. and Dick, S. (2007) *Serves you right.* http:/stonewall.org.uk [accessed: 19/12/09]

Innes, A. (2009) *Dementia Studies.* London: Sage

Jones, K. (2002) The turn of a narrative knowing of persons: one method explored. *Nursing Times Research,* 8, 1: 60-71

Jordan, B. & Jordan, C. (2000), *Tough Love as Social Policy*. London: Sage

Kaplan, L. (2001) A couplehood typology for spouses of institutionalised persons with Alzheimer's disease: perceptions of 'we' – 'I'. *Family Relations,* 50 (1): 87-98

Keady, J., & Nolan, M.R. (2003) The dynamics of dementia: working together, working separately, or working alone? in M.R. Nolan, U. Lundh, G. Grant, & J. Keady (eds.), *Partnerships in family care: understanding the caregiving career.* Maidenhead: Open University Press, pp.15-33.

Kemp, R., Minns, C., Tallack, C., Tilsey, P., Faulkner, D., Marks, I. (2011) Local Authority Cuts. *The Times,* 10th February, p.27

Kitwood, T. (1997) *Dementia Re-considered.* Buckinghamshire: Open University

Knott, C. & Scragg, T. (2010) *Reflective Practice in Social Work* (2nd ed). Exeter: Learning Matters

Lafrance, M. & Stoppard, J. (2007) Re-storying women's depression: A material-discursive approach, in: C. Brown & T. Augusta-Scott (eds) *Narrative Therapy.* Calfornia: Sage. pp.23-37

Lakey, L. (2009) *Counting the Cost.* London: Alzheimer's Society

Lavin, N. (2008) Care settings and the home, in: A. Fannin, L. Fenge, C. Hicks, N. Lavin &K. Brown (2008) *Social Work Practice with Older Lesbians and Gay Men.* Exeter: Learning Matters, pp.51-65

Lawrence, S. & Simpson, G. (2009) International aspects of social work with elders, in: S. Lawrence, K. Lyons, G. Simpson, N. Huegler (eds) *Introducing International Social Work.*Exeter: Learning Matters, pp.76-91

Leamy, M. & Clough, R. (2006) *How Older People Became Researchers.* York: Joseph Rowntree

Letherby, G. (2002) Childless and bereft? Stereotypes and realities in relation to 'voluntary' and 'involuntary' childlessness and womanhood, *Sociological Inquiry,* 72 (1): 7-20

—. (2004) Quoting and counting: an autobiographical response to Oakley, *Sociology,* 38 (1): 175-189

—. (2004) Reply to Ann Oakley, *Sociology,* 38 (1): 193-194

—. (2011) Auto/Biographical reflections on personal and other legacies: much more than money, *Auto/Biography Yearbook,* 2010: 1-20

Liamputtong, P.(2007) *Researching the Vulnerable,* London: Sage

Lipinska, D. (2009) *Person-Centred Counselling for People with Dementia.* London: Jessica Kingsley

Lishman, J. (2009) *Communication in Social Work* (2nd ed). Basingstoke: Palgrave

Lloyd, L. (2003) Caring relationships: looking beyond welfare categories of "carers" and "service users", in: K. Stalker (ed.), *Reconceptualisisng Work with 'Carers'*. London: Jessica Kinglsey, pp. 37-55

Mackenzie, J. (2006) Stigma and dementia: East European and South Asian family carers negotiating stigma in the UK, *Dementia*, 5 (2): 233-247

Malin, N., Wilmot, S. & Manthorpe, J. (2002) *Key Concepts and Debates in Health and Social Policy*. Berkshire: Open University Press

Malseed, J. (2004) Strawmen: a note on Ann Oakley's treatment of text book prescriptions for interviewing, in: C. Searle (2004) *Social Research Methods a Reader*. London: Routledge, pp.261-275

Malthouse, M. (2011) An autoethnography on shifting relationships between a daughter, her mother and Alzheimer's dementia (in any order), *Dementia*, 10(2): 249-256

Manthorpe, J. & Price, E, (2005) Lesbian carers, personal issues and policy responses. *Social Policy and Society*, 5:1: 15-26

Marriott, H. (2003) *The Selfish Pig's Guide to Caring*. Leominster: Polperro Heritage Press

Martin, J. (2007) *Safeguarding Adults*. Dorset: Russell House Publishing

McLaughlin, H. (2007) *Understanding Social Work Research*. London: Sage

Means, R., Richards, S. & Smith, R. (2008) *Community Care* (4th ed). Basingstoke: Palgrave

Menzies, H. (2009) *Enter Mourning*. Toronto: Key Porter

Merrell, J., Kinsella, F., Murphy, F., Philpin, S. and Alia, A. (2006) Accessibility and equity of health and social care services: exploring the views and experiences of Bangladeshi carers in South Wales, UK, *Health and Social Care in the Community*, 14: 197-205

Moon, J.A. (1999) *Reflection in Learning and Professional Development*. Oxfordshire: Kogan Page

Moore, N. (2000) *How to do Research*, London: Library Association Publishing

Moore, W.R. (2002) Lesbian and gay elders: connecting care providers through a telephone support group, *Journal of Gay and Lesbian Social Services*, 14 (3): 23-41

Morgan, H. and Harris, (2005) Strategies for involving services users in outcomes focused research in: L. Lowes & I. Hulatt (eds), *Involving Service Users in Health and Social Care Research*. Oxfordshire: Routledge, pp.163-170

Morris, J. (1991) *Pride Against Prejudice.* London: The Women's Press

Morris, G. & Morris, J. (2010) *The Dementia Care Workbook.* Maidenhead: Open University Press

National Audit Office (2010) *Improving Dementia Services in England* London: The Stationary Office

National Centre for Social Research (2008) *British Social Attitude Survey* http:/ statistics.gov.uk [accessed 20/12/09]

National Institute for Health and Clinical Excellence and the Social Care Institute for Excellence (2006) *Dementia: Supporting people with dementia and their carers in health and social care.* London: Stationary Office

Netto, R., Goh, J. and Yap,P. (2009) Growing and gaining through caring for a loved one with dementia. *Dementia 8,* 2, 245-262

Newman, R. (2010) Surely the world has changed?' in L. Whitman (ed) (2010) *Telling Tales about Dementia.* London: Jessica Kingsley, pp.145-151

Nolan, M., Davies, S. and Grant, G. (2001) *Working with Older People and Their Families: Key Issues in Policy and Practice.* Buckingham: Open University Press

Norman, I., Redfern, S. Briggs, K. & Askham, J. (2004) Perceptions and management of change by people with dementia and their carers living at home, *Dementia,* 3 (1): 19-44

Oakley, A. (1981) Interviewing women: a contradiction in terms, in: H. Roberts (ed) (1981) *Doing Feminist Research.* London: Kogan Paul, pp.30-61

—. (2004) Response to quoting and counting: an autobiographical response to Oakley, *Sociology,* 38: 191-192

O'Connor, D., Phinney, A., Smith, A., Small, J., Purves, B., Perry, J., Drance, E., Donnelly, M., Chaudhury, H. & Beattie, L. (2007) Personhood in dementia care: developing a research agenda for broadening the vision, *Dementia,* 6 (1): 121-142

Office for National Statistics, (2001) *Census of Population and Housing in England and Wales.* London: Stationary Office

Oliver, M. & Sapley, (2006) *Social Work with Disabled People,* (3rd edition) Basingstoke: Palgrave Macmillan

Perren, S.Schmid, R. & Wettsteing, A. (2006) Caregivers' adaption to change: the impact of increasing impairment of persons suffering from dementia on their caregivers' subjective well-being, *Age and Mental Health,* 10 (5): 539-548

Phillips, J. & Marks, G. (2006) Coming out, coming in: how do dominant discourse around aged care facilities take into account the identities and needs of ageing lesbians? *Gay and Lesbian Issues and Psychology Review,* 2(2): 67-77

Phillips, J., Ray, M. & Marshall, M. (2006) *Social Work with Older People.* (4th edition). Basingstoke: Palgrave

Phillips, M., Knocker, S. (2009) *Opening Doors Evaluation The Story So Far.* London: Age Concern

Pierson, J. & Thomas, M. (2010) *Dictionary of Social Work.* Berkshire: Open University Press

Piiparinen, R. & Whitlatch, C.J. (2011) Existential loss as a determinant to well-being in dementia caregiving dyad: a conceptual model, *Dementia,* 10 (2): 185-201

Pool, J. (2008) *The Pool Activity Level (PAL) Instrument,* (3rd edition). London: Jessica Kingsley

Pransky, J. & McMillen, D.P. (2008) Exploring the true nature of internal resilience. in D. Saleebey (2009) *The Strengths Perspective in Social Work,* (5th edition) USA: Pearson, pp. 240-261

Plummer, K. (2001) *Documents of Life 2.* London: Sage

Price, E.(2008) Pride or prejudice? gay men, lesbians and dementia, *British Journal of Social Work,* 38: 1337-1352

Pring, R. 2000, *Philosophy of Educational Research.* London: Continuum

Pritchard, J. (2007) *Working with Adult Abuse.* London: Jessica Kingsley

Punch, K.F. (2000), *Developing Effective Research Proposals.* London: Sage

Quince, C. (2011) *Support. Stay. Save.* http://www.alzheimers.org.uk [accessed 2/2/11]

Ramsay, K. & Letherby, G. (2006) The experiences of academic non-mothers in the gendered university, *Gender, Work and Organization,* 13 (1): 25-44

Ray, M., Bernard, M. & Phillips, J. (2009) *Critical Issues in Social Work with Older People.* Basingstoke: Palgrave

Richards, S., Donovan, S., Victor, V., & Ross, F. (2007) Standing secure amidst a falling world? Practitioner understandings of old age in responses to a case vignette, *Journal of Interprofessional Care,* 21(3): 335-349

Roberts, B. (2002) *Biographical Research.* Buckingham: Open University Press

Rogers, C. (1980) *A Way of Being.* New York: Houghton Mifflin

Roth, S., Atkinson, D., Nind, M. & Welshman, J. (eds) (2005) *Witnesses to Change, Learning Difficulties and History.* Kidderminster: British Institute of Learning Disabilities

Saleebey, D. (2009) *The Strengths Perspective in Social Work,* (5th edition) USA: Pearson

Sanderson, H., Smull, M. & Harvey, J. (2008) Person centred thinking, in: J. Thompson, J. Kilbane & H. Sanderson (eds), *Person Centred Practice for Professionals.* Berkshire: Open University, pp.47-74

Sarantakos, S. (1997) *Social Research,* Basingstoke: Palgrave

Scholl, J.M. & Sabat, S.R. (2008) Stereotypes, stereotype threat and ageing: implications for the understanding and treatment of people with Alzheimer's disease, *Age and Society,* 28: 103-130

Schön, D. (1983) *The Reflective Practitioner.* USA: Basic Books

Scott, A., Ryan, A., James, I.A. & Mitchell, E.A. (2011) Psychological trauma and fear for personal safety as a result of behaviours that challenge in dementia: the experience of healthcare workers, *Dementia,* 10(2): 257-269

Sheard, D. (2008) *Growing.* London: Alzheimer's Society

—. (2009) *Nurturing.* London: Alzheimer's Society

Silverman, D. (2000) Analyzing talk and text, in: N.K. Denzin & Y.S. Lincoln (eds.) *Handbook of Qualitative Research* Second Edition, London: Sage, pp.821-834

Simons, H. (2009) *Case Study.* London: Sage

Skills for Care (2010) Carers' Common Core Principles. http:/skillsforcare.org.uk [accessed 28/9/10]

Smith, A. and Calvert, J. (2001) *Opening Doors.* London: Age Concern England

Stalker, K. (ed) (2003) *Reconceptualising Work with Carers.* London: Jessica Kingsley

Steedman, C. (1986) *The Landscape for a Good Woman.* London: Virago

Stokes, G. (2008) *And Still the Music Plays.* London: Hawker Publications

Stuckey, J.C. (2003) Faith, aging and dementia. *Dementia,* 2 (3): 337-352

Tanner, D and Harris, J (2008) *Working with Older People.* Abingdon: Routledge.

Teater, B, (2010) *An Introduction to Applying Social Work Theories and Methods.* Maidenhead: Open University

The British Education Research Association.2004, *Revised Guidelines for Educational Research.* http:/bera.ac.uk [accessed: 3/7/10]

The Employment Equality (Age) Regulations (2006) in England, Wales and Scotland. London: The Stationary Office

Thomas, J. (2010) Rage, rage, in L. Whitman (ed) (2010) *Telling Tales about Dementia.* London: Jessica Kingsley. pp. 131-135

Thompson, N. (2001) *Anti-Discriminatory Practice* (3rd ed). Basingstoke: Palgrave

—. (2006) *Anti-Discriminatory Practice* (4th ed). Basingstoke: Palgrave.

—. (2003) *Communication and Language.* Basingstoke: Palgrave

Tolley, C. & Ranzijn, R. (2006) Heternormativity amongst staff of residential aged care facilities, *Gay and Lesbian Issues and Psychology Review,* 2(2): 78-86

Townsend, P. (1957) *The Family Life of Older People.* London: Routledge & Kegan Paul

Turnball, A. (2002) *Opening Doors: The Needs of Older Lesbians and Gay Men.* London: Age Concern:

Twigg, J. & Atkin, K. (1994) *Carers Perceived.* Buckingham: Open University Press

Ungerson,C. (1987) *Policy is Personal: Sex, Gender and Informal Care.* London: Tavistock

Valdés, M. (ed) (1991) *A Ricoeur Reader.* Hertfordshire: Harvester Wheatsheaf

Waines, A. (2004) *The Self-Esteem Journal.* London: Sheldon Press

Walmsley, J. (1993) Explaining, in: P. Shakespeare, D. Atkinson, S. French (eds) *Reflecting on Research Practice,* Buckingham: Open University Press, pp. 36-46

Ward, R., Vass, A. A., Garfield, C., Cybyk, B. (2005) A kiss is still a kiss?. *Dementia,* 4 (1): 49-72

Williamson, T. (2008) *Out of the Shadows.* London: Alzheimer's Society

Witkin, S.L. (2000) An integrative humans rights approach to social research, in: C. Truman, D.M. Mertens, B. Humphries, B. (eds) *Research and Inequality,* London: UCCL, pp. 205-219

University of Southampton (2008) *School of Education Ethical and Governance Review Procedures,* Southampton: School of Education

Zarit, S. & Zarit, J. (2008) Flexibility and change: the fundamentals for families coping with dementia, in M. Downs & B. Bowers (eds), *Excellence in Dementia Care.* Berkshire: Open University Press, pp. 85-103

INDEX